# Taming the *Troublesome* Board Member

By Katha Kissman

BOARDSOURCE®
*Building Effective Nonprofit Boards*

*Library of Congress Cataloging-in-Publication Data*

Kissman, Katha.

  Taming the troublesome board member / by Katha Kissman

    p. cm.

  Includes bibliographical references.
  ISBN 1-58686-081-X (pbk.)

1. Boards of directors. 2. Interpersonal relations.  I. Title.

HD2745.K57 2006
658.4'22--dc22

                         2006024183

**Building Effective Nonprofit Boards**

Formerly the National Center for Nonprofit Boards

BoardSource, formerly the National Center for Nonprofit Boards, is the premier resource for practical information, tools and best practices, training, and leadership development for board members of nonprofit organizations worldwide. Through our highly acclaimed programs and services, BoardSource enables organizations to fulfill their missions by helping build strong and effective nonprofit boards.

BoardSource provides assistance and resources to nonprofit leaders through workshops, training, and our extensive Web site, www.boardsource.org. A team of BoardSource governance consultants works directly with nonprofit leaders to design specialized solutions to meet organizations' needs and assists nongovernmental organizations around the world through partnerships and capacity building. As the world's largest, most comprehensive publisher of materials on nonprofit governance, BoardSource offers a wide selection of books, videotapes, CDs, and online tools. BoardSource also hosts the BoardSource Leadership Forum, bringing together governance experts, board members, and chief executives of nonprofit organizations from around the world.

Created out of the nonprofit sector's critical need for governance guidance and expertise, BoardSource is a 501(c)(3) nonprofit organization that has provided practical solutions to nonprofit organizations of all sizes in diverse communities. In 2001, BoardSource changed its name from the National Center for Nonprofit Boards to better reflect its mission. Today, BoardSource has approximately 11,000 members and has served more than 75,000 nonprofit leaders.

For more information, please visit our Web site, www.boardsource.org, e-mail us at mail@boardsource.org, or call us at 800-883-6262.

# Have You Used These BoardSource Resources?

## VIDEOS

*Meeting the Challenge: An Orientation to Nonprofit Board Service*

*Speaking of Money: A Guide to Fundraising for Nonprofit Board Members*

## BOOKS

*The Board Chair Handbook*

*Managing Conflicts of Interest: A Primer for Nonprofit Boards*

*Driving Strategic Planning: A Nonprofit Executive's Guide*

*The Board-Savvy CEO: How To Build a Strong, Positive Relationship with Your Board*

*Presenting: Board Orientation*

*Presenting: Nonprofit Financials*

*Meet Smarter: A Guide to Better Nonprofit Board Meetings*

*The Board Building Cycle: Nine Steps to Finding, Recruiting, and Engaging Nonprofit Board Members*

*The Nonprofit Policy Sampler, Second Edition*

*To Go Forward, Retreat! The Board Retreat Handbook*

*Nonprofit Board Answer Book: Practical Guide for Board Members and Chief Executives*

*Nonprofit Board Answer Book II: Beyond the Basics*

*The Nonprofit Legal Landscape*

*Self-Assessment for Nonprofit Governing Boards*

*Assessment of the Chief Executive*

*Fearless Fundraising*

*The Nonprofit Board's Guide to Bylaws*

*Understanding Nonprofit Financial Statements*

*Transforming Board Structure: Strategies for Committees and Task Forces*

## THE GOVERNANCE SERIES

1. *Ten Basic Responsibilities of Nonprofit Boards*
2. *Financial Responsibilities of Nonprofit Boards*
3. *Structures and Practices of Nonprofit Boards*
4. *Fundraising Responsibilities of Nonprofit Boards*
5. *Legal Responsibilities of Nonprofit Boards*
6. *The Nonprofit Board's Role in Setting and Advancing the Mission*
7. *The Nonprofit Board's Role in Planning and Evaluation*
8. *How To Help Your Board Govern More and Manage Less*
9. *Leadership Roles in Nonprofit Governance*

For an up-to-date list of publications and information about current prices, membership, and other services, please call BoardSource at 800-883-6262 or visit our Web site at www.boardsource.org.

# Contents

# Acknowledgements

I wish to thank the numerous individuals who have helped me in my research and brainstorming about this topic. A very special thanks to three longtime friends and mentors: Dick Snowdon, who for this book and for years always has just the right story and the right words to get a point across; Catherine Irwin, for the gift of lessons on building community and stewardship versus ego; and Joyce Henderson, for the benefit of her critical eye, deep knowledge, vast experience, and eternally positive presence.

Special thanks to the team at BoardSource, especially Marla Bobowick and Karen Hansen. And without Claire Perella's diligence, insights, and brilliance, the final product would not be half of what it is. I deeply appreciate all her help and good cheer.

This text builds on previous ideas and the author sincerely thanks Maureen Robinson for the benefit of her work and thoughts on the many different kinds of "trouble," and for reminding us that a troublesome board can be a very different animal than a troublesome board member (or a few). Additionally, thank you to Mark Bailey, author of the previous BoardSource publication, *The Troublesome Board Member*.

A loving thank you to Alvin R. Kissman, Gerald Kissman, and Rick Reitz for making sure I had a beautiful new Asclepian in which to heal — think, dream, research, and write. To Elise Yanker I offer my gratitude for deepening my understanding of team theory and how applicable it is to almost everything in life. And to those others I am grateful to have met and know in the human journey, who gave freely of time, insights, stories, and help: Jan Adamec, Gayle Anderson, Naseer Aruri, Bernice Bass de Martinez, Deborah A. Bricker, Brian Carpenter, Jane Cohen, Carolyn Coleman, Cheryl Cooper, Kae Dakin, Julie Danis, Fran D'Ooge, Tom DiGiovanni, Lynne Friedmann, Deborah Milstein Gardner, Bryant George, Chuck Gould, Mary Gray, Frances Hesselbein, Nadia Hijab, Leslie Hindman, Cheryl Kagan, Brian Kissman, Dave Kissman, Nadra D. Kissman, Rachel Kraft, Peter Jablow, the women of Leadership America, Cindy Lewin, Karla Madison, Alicia Mullen, Collette Murray, Jeanne Oakes, Eliot Pfanstiehl, Margaret Poole, Lana Porter, Ane Powers, Rebecca Rush, David Sadd, Richard C. Shadyac, Sr., Ruth Ann Skaff, Jeffrey Slavin, Patricia Stocker, Volunteers of America, Lisa Werner, Jerry Whiddon, and those several others who specifically asked to remain anonymous.

I dedicate this book to the memory of my late husband, Samih K. Farsoun, who taught me much about integrity, respecting others, living life well, and the ultimate power of love.

Finally, I offer: No one is perfect. No one gets it right every time. But it is in the trying, the learning of lessons, the exchange of kindness, and the celebrating of successes together that the world is made better.

# Foreword

This book is long overdue. Over the 30 years that I have been actively engaged in philanthropy, the nonprofit boardroom has undergone a dramatic and often unpleasant change. The days of the genteel, collegial, deferential board of trustees is long since gone. In one sense this is both good and necessary. It can surely be said that many nonprofit boards of the past failed to fully discharge their obligations as trustees. I, for one, plead guilty. Too often we simply rubber-stamped what management recommended and failed to challenge decisions that should have been tested. With management misconduct in both the for-profit and nonprofit world, a higher standard of oversight is absolutely the order of the day. While there are unfortunate examples where trustees have used this revived sense of responsibility to act in inappropriate ways, in most cases, trustees now understand that higher threshold and are raising the bar in the most appropriate ways.

It's those unfortunate examples that beg further diligence. Some trustees have come from a for-profit world where they have often been extraordinarily successful and have thought that their receipts for business success could be translated into the nonprofit world without understanding the important, but often subtle, differences. Others have come to a nonprofit board without an adequate understanding of the organization or having clear mutual expectations with behavior flowing from misunderstanding. Finally, there is a group (however small) that comes with a personal agenda. It is this latter group that can be the most troubling because no amount of education is likely to move its motivation from a personal desire to institutional priority.

What Katha Kissman has done is lay out a blueprint for avoiding and resolving the problem of disruptive board members. It is a process that must start with asking a very difficult question: "Are they right?" How off-putting and boorish the behavior, on the substance they may be right. If that is the case, the problem is the institution's, not the board members'. If they are wrong, then you need to understand why. Good-faith disagreement is quite different from a personal agenda.

This book helps to avoid troublesome behavior by reminding us of the need for proper selection and orientation. It helps deal with the problems that do surface from those mistakes. And finally, it helps identify and resolve the individual troublesome behavior problem quickly and with as much grace as possible. This should be required reading not only for every nominating, governance, or trusteeship committee, but should be compulsory reading for every board member.

Richard W. Snowdon, III
*The Hill-Snowdon Foundation, Washington, DC*

# Introduction

The Cambridge Dictionary defines *trouble* as difficulties stemming from a characteristic of someone or something that is considered a disadvantage or problem. *Trouble* could be a situation in which problems or difficulties result from something that has been done or something that has failed to operate as it should. At the extreme, *trouble* could be problems of malfeasance, or could result in arguments, fighting, or violence. *Troubling* is something that causes distress, worry, or anxiety. It may not actually be *trouble* yet, but a red flag that might require attention or intervention.

*Troubles* or something that initially starts out as *troubling* can lead to **troublesome**. *Troublesome* describes something or someone that causes action or inaction, problems or difficulties. These actions or behaviors can be temporary or chronic, mild and just plain irritating, or serious enough to cause great and lasting damage if not addressed in a timely manner.

Chief executives, board chairs, and consultants constantly seek solutions to the multitude of challenges a nonprofit board may face at any juncture. The short- or long-term effects of an individual board member's troublesome actions or behaviors can be one of the greatest detriments to this leadership team. These effects can be both direct — confusion, loss of energy or focus, difficulty in making decisions — and indirect — weakened morale, loss of productivity and service quality, and in extreme cases, high board or staff turnover and a damaged public reputation.

The first step in finding a successful resolution to difficulties with an individual is recognizing that a person's actions or behaviors usually stem from something specific, whether it is ignorance, misunderstanding, a personality conflict, or a deeper issue. This is predicated on the assumption that a second step will occur — that leadership will intervene directly, humanely, with unity, and in a timely way. If leadership doesn't guide the process, the trouble could be left unattended and may result in disaster. The final step, finding a winning solution, will require unique approaches for different groups and various answers for differing circumstances. In some cases it may involve looking at board structure to affect a minor change in board process, or a major culture shift of the entire board. In other cases it will necessitate "holding up the mirror" to help the individual take a step back and understand the effects of his or her behavior within the context of the board's work, and provide suggestions for change. And yes, the ultimate solution might also mean a change in board membership — asking a board member to give up his or her seat on the board.

Easier said than done, right? Why? Because boards are made up of people. No one enjoys conflict or confrontation, especially with regard to a professional colleague. Successfully working in a group context is highly dynamic and can engender great passion and emotion when disagreements or conflicts erupt. Paying attention to these dynamics and actively honoring the human element requires commitment and work. M. Scott Peck, M.D., in *The Road Less Traveled*, reminds us:

> *…That process of confronting and solving problems is a painful one.*
> *Problems, depending upon their nature, evoke in us frustration or grief or*

*sadness or loneliness or guilt or regret or anger or fear or anxiety or anguish or despair. These are uncomfortable feelings ... Fearing the pain involved, almost all of us, to a greater or lesser degree, attempt to avoid problems. We procrastinate, hoping that they will go away. We ignore them, forget them, pretend they do not exist . . . We attempt to skirt around problems rather than meet them head on.*[1]

Effective communication and positive conflict resolution are easiest to achieve when people treat each other with dignity and respect. It is under this overarching concept that *Taming the Troublesome Board Member* provides strategies, tips, and tools to build an understanding of how to partner with or disengage from troublesome board members to eliminate the unnecessary barriers to the ongoing effectiveness of the nonprofit board.

## ABOUT THE BOOK

Case study examples are used throughout this book to illustrate troublesome behaviors and provide analysis and recommendations. Many of these cases are based on real-life situations. The author has created composites from them and taken artistic license to underscore meaning.

The reader should note that the author has categorized and labeled behaviors for the purposes of convenience. The author realizes these categories are imperfect in that different behaviors could be grouped in different ways. These particular categories have been created for ease of understanding in the context of board work.

Chapter 1 further discusses the need to understand the problem before it can be solved, providing information on the realities of group work, the framework for the discussion of troublesome behaviors, and considerations for how to avoid troublesome board members. The behaviors addressed in Chapter 2 are those that have been categorized as displaying poor "boardmanship," stemming from failure to perform the job well. Many of these behaviors could have been prevented with proper recruitment and orientation; most can be addressed with timely recognition and direct intervention. Chapter 3 addresses behaviors that are tied more closely to people skills (or lack thereof) or conflicted personality characteristics. These may or may not be fixable. Some unique troubles have been introduced in Chapter 4, addressing those behaviors that defy easy categorization but which many organizations have faced at one time or another. Most of these circumstances warrant an even more delicate approach to solutions, and possibly a need for additional professional advice and/or alternative leadership solutions. Chapter 5 offers final thoughts on the human realities that should be embraced by all to avoid troublesome.

## AUTHOR'S NOTE TO THE READER

As I started writing this book, I made the assumption that I would not have to remind the reader that most troublesome behavior results from certain failures in the recruitment/nomination process of and orientation process for new board members.

---

1.  Peck, M. Scott, M.D. *The Road Less Traveled*. New York: Simon & Schuster, 1978. Page 16.

Or that not having up-to-date bylaws, a board manual, a regularly reviewed and signed conflict-of-interest policy, or a code of ethics contributes to these challenges as well. Or that ongoing, continuing education for board development is extremely important, and regular assessment along with stated recourse mechanisms is absolutely imperative. To my surprise, I found that the vast majority of the examples and case studies I received directly resulted from these failures. Most surprising was that **it was readily acknowledged that boards had not done this work due to time constraints or fear of insulting already-courted board member candidates.** Therefore, many of these mandates are mentioned within this text so that *all* of the practices and strategies for dealing with troublesome boards and board members are in one place between two covers.

It is anticipated that the average person picking up this book is seeking advice for addressing the effects of a specific behavior in the boardroom. Therefore, the book is organized as a reference guide to provide this ready and selected access. Reading the book cover to cover and reviewing each and every behavior back to back, while flattering to the author, may actually discourage someone from staying on a board (may this not be so!). Rather, the author hopes and trusts that the seeker will find a bit of wit and wisdom overall and practical help in the specific as may be needed.

It is also likely that the reader may be the chief executive or a consultant seeking to address the behaviors of a troublesome board member. Consultants may find specific preventions and solutions when dealing with troublesome behavior, and they may be called upon to coach a board chair in how to set the stage and say the words to address these behaviors calmly, rationally, and humanely. But to be most effective, consultants should be invited to do so by the board chair, not the chief executive. At times the chief executive is the first to recognize a problem and may be most impacted by such behaviors, yet must be careful in his or her criticism of board members. A chief executive certainly can benefit from the contents of this book in an effort to understand what might be happening, but ultimately it is not the chief executive's responsibility to take on the fix. It is the role of the board chair.

I fervently hope that board chairs will find this book empowering and accessible as they are the ones who need to take action; and whenever possible, to do so without the aid of a consultant. While I believe in the ability of a consultant to provide intervention and assistance, in the case of one-on-ones, I'd rather go out of business as a consultant encouraging, "Physician, heal thyself." When the troublesome behavior comes from the board leadership, other board members need to take it on. Again, this is not the chief executive's role.

I hope that the timely reminder and the consciousness-raising about the need to look hard at how the board processes and provides empathy will help board leaders to recognize, intervene, and find the right solution for each situation. The pages that follow will emphasize the commonality of these problems, provide objective analysis from my many years spent in the boardroom, and will serve as a reminder of promising practices while adding the human touch.

# Chapter 1: Understanding the Problem

Recognition of troublesome board member behaviors usually starts like this:

*"Joe came on like a dynamo, promising this and promising that, especially large sums of money. When it became clear to all of us that he just wasn't going to come through and that some of his promises were actually costing the organization money, we knew we needed to do something."*

*"Why does Evelyn need to revisit each and every issue, even when we made definite decisions about some of these issues months ago? She just won't let up, even when she is the lone dissenter on a vote!"*

*"I hate to say it, but Ginny has a personal agenda on this board. I can't believe that others don't notice this. Sometimes her recommendations are really not in the best interests of the whole, but rather in the best interests of Ginny."*

Usually recognition is *not* the biggest challenge. Battling the fear of intervention and finding the best solutions are what hamper most boards.

Troublesome behaviors are tricky. No two situations are alike and each case can have layers of complexity that contribute to the overall negative effect. What may start out as short-term troubling behaviors can become chronic troublesome behaviors if not recognized or actively ignored. Addressing troubling behavior in a timely manner can make the difference between troubling and troublesome. And, understanding the root of troublesome behaviors is critical to finding the best way to change or overcome the situation. Some of these behaviors can be managed to save the person's seat on the board. Some can be managed but it may not be the best course of action. Some simply cannot, and should not, be managed and action to remove a board member should be taken as quickly as possible.

## MULTIPLE SIDES OF "TROUBLE"

A board can be *in* trouble and can feel like trouble to a board chair or chief executive but not really be *troublesome*. Among other things, a board in trouble cannot find people willing to join it, doesn't know who best to fill the board chair seat, has trouble managing a quorum, and is not willing to deal with troublesome members. These boards suffer from a general apathy and lack of focus, but will most likely respond to good leadership and the introduction of more disciplined and productive practices if provided.

Boards that seem troubling to their leaders may be a healthy response to a chair who is too controlling, an executive committee that has become too powerful, or a chief executive who is falling short in a variety of ways — lack of vision, poor communication with the board, shoddy management, and unreliable judgment. Periodically acting out in a demanding or high-maintenance way is not the worst thing a board could do, especially if it might result in higher levels of accountability, engagement, and performance. Consider the following illustration:

Linda Lear was asked to serve on the board of a regional organization some time ago. She joined the board at a time when there was only one other female out of 15 board members. All members of the board, including Linda, were Caucasian. Linda felt that the board composition should really change, but she vowed to wait and find natural and constructive opportunities in which to raise the flag.

She'd been on the board for almost eight months when she received her meeting package for next week's meeting. The governance committee's new slate of board candidates included five white males, all from the corporate sector. She picked up the phone and called her friend, another board member, who had nominated her in the first place.

---

---

**Linda:** "Exactly what kind of organization did I join, Bill? Did you see the nominating committee's list? This doesn't really reflect the composition of the community we serve, does it?"

At the meeting, Bill opened up a discussion of the slate and suggested that they table a few nominees for a future slate and use this opportunity to increase the diversity of the board. The other board members were a little surprised, but then sincerely agreed that it was a good idea. The brainstorming was fun and exciting — several alternate candidates from the community were suggested and there were quite a number of highly qualified individuals. The slate was eventually revised to include an African-American woman who was vice president of a local financial institution, and two other women, one who ran a very successful nonprofit and another who was a former professor and now a community activist. They all accepted their candidacy and were all voted in.

Later, the board was discussing whether or not to support a local initiative that would benefit the local Hispanic/Latino community. In this region, that community segment wasn't very large, but it was growing fast and they needed specific help for job skills training.

**Randy:** "Maybe we should hold off supporting them to see if they actually stay in business. No sense giving our money to a group that may not be viable."

**Linda:** *"Gee — it's not really 'our' money, Randy. It's money we've been entrusted with to do good in the community, isn't it? But more importantly, how do you think they are going to gain viability? Maybe our funding would make the difference between this organization thriving or dying."*

*The funding was granted.*

*Later that year, when there was a discussion about an issue for increased school funding to which Linda's organization wasn't asked to contribute but to take a public position of support, George made a laughing comment:*

*"Well, I guess we should do it. But we better be careful supporting these kinds of issues — we might look like we are in favor of increasing government spending to all kinds of social causes. We don't want to have tons of air-headed liberals knocking on our door."*

*Linda said, also laughing: "Gee, George. You better be careful. I am one of those air-headed liberals and I think there are a couple more of us sitting around this table."*

*Everyone laughed. But the point was taken.*

Sometimes it takes one or a few change agents who may at first look like trouble, but who actually help the board look in the mirror. In this case, Linda was strategic and worked the system at the appropriate times to encourage changes that made sense and to initiate a little consciousness-raising for her fellow board members.

Troublesome *boards* are different, however. They replace apathy with negativity and create obstacles to a reasonable resolution of difficulties or disagreements. Troublesome boards are dominated by cliques and factions; they take problems into the community, lowering the confidence of their stakeholders; they frequently clash with the staff and create a climate that pushes chief executives out.

Boards in trouble or troublesome boards need intervention and will often require outside help from a trained facilitator or consultant to guide the group in working through its trouble. If the reader believes that he or she is dealing with a board in trouble or a troublesome board as a whole, solutions will lie in analyzing and reworking the structural elements of the board, such as mission articulation, leadership delegation and accountabilities, collective roles and responsibilities, bylaws, committee structure, and other board processes, as well as methodologies to increase board engagement. While these structural elements may, and in many cases will, overlap with the context of this book, please note that these chapters are not designed to specifically address broader systemic and structural challenges. What this book is designed to do is to help with recognizing, intervening, and solving troublesome behaviors of an individual board member.

## WHAT IS AT THE ROOT OF THE PROBLEM?

First, the full board needs to take a step back and assess whether or not it contributed to or created the problem. Before addressing the behaviors of an individual, the board must do its homework and ask some very hard questions of itself as a body: Did we recruit well? Was this person brought on the board for the right reasons? Did this person receive an adequate onboarding?

## What Is Onboarding?

*Onboarding* is a global term used in this context for properly introducing, orienting, installing, and welcoming someone into organizational culture. It is both formal and informal and requires active sensitivity and an ongoing human touch. In response to proper onboarding, turnover is highly reduced and team restructuring is more successful. The term is actually used in the corporate sector more than in the nonprofit sector, which may seem ironic since nonprofits tend to be more conscious of doing the work to make sure someone is satisfied with his or her decision to join "the cause." *Onboarding* is most often used in the context of teamwork and in understanding the need to move to the productive stage quickly when new teams are formed or existing teams experience a transition.

Generally, troublesome behaviors of an individual stem from

- the board's failure in the recruitment, orientation, and onboarding of a new board member
- the new board member's failure to understand the legal obligations that come with being a board member
- the new board member's failure to embrace the nature of board work as teamwork
- the board's and the individual's failure to manage personal issues or special cases so that they do not impact the board governance process

## FAILURE TO RECRUIT, ORIENT, AND ONBOARD PROPERLY

Board members are recruited to serve on a board for a variety of reasons:

- People are committed to or have a passion for the mission of the organization.
- People can bring added value to the board team due to a particular and needed expertise, skill, or experience.
- People have a personal or professional profile that can add legitimacy and credibility to the organization.
- People can bring money and connections to other individuals and organizations.

While the above are very important considerations when recruiting specific board members, it is important to also take the following criteria into consideration in order to avoid "troublesome":

- people who will be on their best behavior
- people who have excellent "people skills"
- people who are committed to doing group work
- people who understand, respect, and fulfill their stated roles and responsibilities

Often the recruitment and nomination process does not go deep enough to uncover whether or not a potential board member is capable of bringing the last four criteria to the board table. Troublesome behavior can also surface if a new board member was not educated enough in advance about roles and responsibilities, board process, or board culture. This leads to a lack of understanding on the new board member's part, and will not only impact the effectiveness of the particular individual's contributions, but also the efficiency of the board's work as a whole. Additionally, having expectations of someone who is not clear about those expectations is not only unproductive but unfair and, in this context, unprofessional.

## Recruiting Board Members for the *Wrong* Reasons

Sometimes troublesome behaviors are inadvertently invited onto a board because the wrong people are recruited for the wrong reasons.

*"My friend Jack is a great guy. I just know he'd be great on our board. I don't think he knows much about our organization, but he can get to know it once he joins."*

*"Ms. Smith has lots of money. Let's ask her to be on our board."*

*"Rose said she would be happy to come on our board. We need her because she is so known in the community and having her name on our letterhead would do a lot for us. But I had to promise her that she wouldn't have to come to meetings."*

*"George is on the Zoo board and I've heard he has raised a lot of money for the organization. He really doesn't like to go to plays, but we should have him on our theatre board anyway because if he raised money for the Zoo he should be able to raise money for us."*

Scenarios like these are played out over and over again, and effective boards address these risks actively within their board development process. Some of the above reasons for wanting an individual to serve may be valid, but ultimately, these reasons must fit within the entire context of an overall process for candidate review.

---

### FOOD FOR THOUGHT

Someone who may seem like a good board member for all the right reasons may be wrong simply because he or she is overcommitted.

*"I have and do serve on several boards in the Chicago area. I feel like it's an important civic duty. However, I have had to do some soul searching. I only have so much time in the day and I didn't want my effectiveness in anything I do to be compromised by being stretched too thin. My New Year's resolution was to limit my time spent on nonprofit work to two hours a day. This means I have had to learn to say no, promptly and directly, to many things (including being asked to serve on new nonprofit boards), in order to bring better quality to those commitments I have already made. I believe that in the case of the nonprofits, it allows them to find others who can truly commit to their work in a way I might not be able to at the time."*

Leslie Hindman, Leslie Hindman Auctioneers, Chicago, IL

---

## Providing Purpose to Board Work

Sometimes, even the most seasoned and experienced board member is troubled. In *Governance as Leadership*, the authors address "troublesome" in a different way. They say that "many board members are ineffectual not just because they are confused by their role but because they are dissatisfied with their roles. They do not do their job well because their job does not strike them as worth doing well."[2]

Labeled as the problem of purpose, it may be a far vaster issue contributing to troublesome behavior than one might think. The authors of *Governance as Leadership* maintain that the four contributors to this problem of purpose are

1. Some official work is highly episodic.

2. Some official work is intrinsically unsatisfying.

3. Some important unofficial work is undemanding.

4. Some unofficial work is rewarding but discouraged.

---

**NECESSARY KNOWLEDGE**

**Official vs. Unofficial Work**

*Official work*: Governing through the use of authority to set an organization's purposes and to ensure it serves those purposes effectively and efficiently.

*Unofficial work*: Informal coaching of a chief executive, advising and troubleshooting with staff outside of board meetings, volunteering on the front lines of service delivery.[3]

---

Board member satisfaction absolutely relates to board effectiveness. Clearly stating the expectations to potential board nominees may weed out those for whom the nature of the work is not their cup of tea or something they simply aren't willing to do. If a potential board member understands the nature of the work — both the challenging and the mundane — before even coming on board, he or she is more likely to find purpose and meaning because it was agreed to up front.

Unless there is a common understanding of meaning, the problem of purpose can and will contribute to troublesome behaviors. In some cases, individuals choose board service because they are seeking something to fulfill the personal need to create meaning or legacy. This is an admirable quality in board members. Or sometimes it's because they simply want something to do. In the right context, this can also be quite desirable. Where it becomes troublesome is when what a board member thinks should be done or what he or she may want to personally do on

---

2.  Chait, Richard P., William P. Ryan, and Barbara E. Taylor. *Governance as Leadership: Reframing the Work of Nonprofit Boards*. Co-published by BoardSource, Washington, DC; and John Wiley & Sons, Inc., New York, 2005.

3.  Ibid.

behalf of the organization is not consistent with the strategic plan, is a contrary articulation of the organization's mission, or is actually part of day-to-day operations instead of necessary oversight.

---

### FOOD FOR THOUGHT

*"I believe good board orientation and continuing leadership development opportunities for board members responsible for governance help avoid most troublesome situations and behaviors."*

Frances Hesselbein, Chairman, Leader to Leader Institute, New York, NY

---

### FAILURE TO UNDERSTAND LEGAL OBLIGATIONS

The vast majority of nonprofit board members understand that being a member of a board of directors carries specific legal responsibilities and fiduciary obligations to ensure the organization is carrying out its mission in a responsible manner, both operationally and financially. Board members are responsible for protecting the organization from legal action, promoting safe and ethical working conditions for staff, and safeguarding the organization's integrity.[4] No one would argue that this is what a board member does, or should do. "Troublesome" enters the picture when an individual board member does not actively remember that his or her presence on the board and participation as a board member carries these legal and ethical responsibilities, and therefore, fails to live up to them.

If this type of troublesome behavior is not addressed, an organization runs the risk of facing serious legal and financial trouble from which it may never recover. In light of the corporate scandals of the late 1990s and early 2000s, Congress has taken a keen interest and stronger position on preventing these situations in the future. Toward this end, the Sarbanes-Oxley Act of 2002 introduced new requirements for publicly traded companies in the corporate sector to broaden the board's governance role in financial and auditing procedures. Although only two provisions of the Act apply specifically to nonprofit organizations, Sarbanes-Oxley has been a wake-up call for nonprofits. All nonprofits should discuss the following practices and their relevance to their own policies and processes:

- independent audits and the establishment of an audit committee

- requirements and standards of auditors

- certification of financial statements by chief executives and chief financial officers

---

4.  Dambach, Charles F., Oliver Tessier, and Carol E. Weisman. *The Business Professional's Guide to Nonprofit Board Service*. Washington, DC: BoardSource, 2002.

- avoidance of making personal loans to directors or executives; or if provided, the loans must be approved by the board, the process for providing the loan should be documented, and the value and terms of the loan should be disclosed

- enforcing a conflict-of-interest policy in which board members annually disclose their potential conflicts of interest

- compliance with the timeliness, accuracy, and completeness of the Forms 990 or 990-PF by filing electronically when that option is available to them

- greater disclosure and transparency of financial position

- development, adoption, and disclosure in a formal process to deal with complaints and prevent retaliation

- a whistleblower policy for taking employee and volunteer complaints seriously, investigating each situation, and protecting the concerned individual from undue punishment for disclosing a concern

- written document retention and periodic destruction policy

Already, a few proactive states are considering or have passed legislature applying the spirit of Sarbanes-Oxley to their nonprofit organizations (most notably, California's Nonprofit Integrity Act of 2004). A key responsibility for current and future nonprofit boards will be to keep their antennae up with regard to further developments and the impacts on the sector.

But even the most conscious, transparent, accountable board cannot fully prevent troublesome board behavior. Is it something else?

## FOOD FOR THOUGHT

*"In light of the current emphasis on accountability and transparency in the nonprofit sector, it has become even more important for board members to take their roles very seriously. However, the role does not include 'managing' the organization or undermining board decisions. Ideally, the board and senior leadership participate in a 'shared governance' of the organization and it takes time and patience to work together to achieve that. There are many professionals available who can provide the proper training and mentoring to boards and the key is that it is done in partnership with the chief executive and executive staff. As board members begin to more clearly understand their role as a trustee there is a good chance that negative behaviors will be minimized."*

Colette M. Murray, J.D., CFRE, Paschal Murray, Inc., Executive Search, San Diego, CA

*"Board members often lose sight of how much volunteer work they perform for an organization at the expense of their policy-setting role. I once tracked this for a year and was genuinely surprised to find that the majority of my time for one organization was spent in volunteer activities. I discussed this with my board president, and asked, 'Am I more valuable to you as a volunteer or as a board member, because I can't be both?' Once we agreed that my role was that of policy setting, it became much easier to deflect volunteer assignments. I'm now a more focused and productive board member."*

Lynne Friedmann, Friedmann Communications, Solana Beach, CA

## FAILURE TO EMBRACE BOARD WORK AS TEAMWORK

Being part of a team requires commitment to group work. It warrants a special understanding of group dynamics and often a control of certain behaviors for the betterment of the team. When board members commit to board service, they also commit to group work, or teamwork. Often, *trouble* on a board stems from the failure of an individual to understand his or her place on the team; or a troublesome behavior may result as a byproduct of team development. Understanding the basics of team theory can help in recognizing and resolving situational troublesome behavior.

Referring to the groundbreaking work of Bruce W. Tuckman, whenever a group of individuals comes together for a common purpose, they form a team. Tuckman's model suggests that every team goes through five developmental stages: 1) forming, 2) storming, 3) norming, 4) performing, and 5) adjourning.

While these stages can flow from one to the other, internal and external impacts might readily move a team backward or forward by one or two stages. In the context of nonprofit boards, examples of nonlinear progression may come from the addition of a new board member, a change in board leadership, a term ending or resignation of a board member, a chief executive transition, or an organizational crisis. At each stage, teams display various behaviors and team members experience different feelings. With each different feeling or behavior, the productivity of the team is affected.

Tuckman provides the following model[5]:

| Stages of Team Development | | | |
|---|---|---|---|
| STAGE | BEHAVIORS | FEELINGS | PRODUCTIVITY |
| **Forming** | • Attempts to define the task<br>• Attempts to determine team norms<br>• Focus on the "self" as opposed to the team<br>• Polite<br>• High-level discussions<br>• Team members testing the leader<br>• Complaints<br>• Discussions about why "it" won't work | • Nervous<br>• Pride for being selected<br>• Excitement<br>• Optimism<br>• Fear<br>• Anxiety | • Low |
| **Storming** | • Arguing<br>• Differences of opinion<br>• Defensiveness<br>• Quietness<br>• Interruptions<br>• Team members not listening<br>• Round and round discussion | • Resistance<br>• Fluctuations and shifts in attitude toward the team or task<br>• Frustration | • Low |
| **Norming** | • Attempts to reduce conflict<br>• More personal sharing and confiding in each other<br>• Team norms are respected<br>• A shift in the focus from the self to the team | • A sense of team spirit and camaraderie<br>• Acceptance as a team member<br>• Relief that work will get done | • Medium |
| **Performing** | • Individuals begin looking at their behaviors and self-adjusting<br>• Team solves problems together<br>• Supportiveness and attachment within the team | • Satisfaction with work<br>• Energized<br>• Sense of belonging | • High |
| **Adjourning** | • Closure<br>• Celebration | • Sadness<br>• Pride of accomplishment | |

5.  Tuckman, Bruce W. "Development Sequence in Small Groups." *Psychological Bulletin*, 1965. Volume 63 (6).

If the natural progression of a team in development is the cause of trouble, this troublesome behavior may not last. It can be acknowledged as a response to group dynamics at a particular time or due to a particular situation. Recognition of the potential cause of these behaviors or feelings will clear a path for the team to move into a more productive stage where high performance and cohesiveness can replace inconsistencies and feelings of resistance.

A nonprofit board is a team formed to serve a specific mission purpose. It is different from a workplace team or a sports team in that relationships are developed and maintained only in the context of meetings and communication in between those meetings. For these relative strangers that come together only four to six times a year, adapting to complex group dynamics while serving the mission, dealing with organizational goals, and making important decisions in a limited amount of time requires strong leadership, focus, and heartfelt work on the part of every individual involved. Not only do board members contribute their valuable time and expertise, but they must make a commitment to understanding relationships, learning to trust, and accepting a common purpose.

Keeping these complex layers of board commitment in mind, it is true that boards tend to blow off feelings or behaviors expressed because those feelings or behaviors might not have a direct impact on each team member's episodic board work since the board team is not physically connected on a daily basis. When a board does not actively acknowledge or deal with occasional behaviors, it might still be able to do its work and be productive. But feelings or behaviors could escalate far more rapidly and with greater intensity because of the artificial nature of the team. The energy required to work through these episodes is usually unwarranted and exhausting. In an attempt to avoid the extra work, fellow board members will silently rationalize that in the long run it probably won't matter — after all, everybody is serving on the board for the right reasons. They were nominated in the first place, weren't they? This kind of reaction must be guarded against; instead, a proactive understanding and application of team theory can be of enormous assistance if employed on a regular basis to keep understandable team responses from growing into troublesome board behavior.

As part of team theory, the board's composition and responsibilities may change at each phase of the organization's lifecycle, with potential for troublesome behaviors to result from the nonprofit's move from one phase to the next. For example, in a start-up organization, board members are often the individuals who are also the unpaid or minimally paid staff. They provide the day-to-day management of mission delivery and governance is often intertwined with the other necessary work at hand. As an organization matures and hires paid, professional staff, day-to-day management is no longer the board's job. The work of the board, therefore, turns its focus exclusively to policymaking, strategic thinking, and oversight. Troublesome behaviors often stem directly from the lack of understanding that as an organization changes and matures, requirements of individual board members may shift.

## FOOD FOR THOUGHT

Chuck Gould, National President and CEO of Volunteers of America, Inc., addressed what is not so much a behavior as it is a phenomenon leading to behaviors, that can present trouble in the context of a national organization with affiliate chapters.

Chuck has been a part of Volunteers of America practically his entire life. His grandparents and parents were involved and, as a young boy, Chuck was an active volunteer. Even before he became the chief executive, Chuck saw a dichotomy in this particular nonprofit model of a national headquarters with local affiliates or organizational members serving as board members: representatives from outside the organization (experts and advocates who believe in Volunteers of America's ministry of service) and inside the organization (chief executives of Volunteers of America's affiliate organizations) were serving on the national board of directors. Chuck notes:

*"I think it's just a process of consciousness-raising — reminding people of the need to fulfill their responsibilities at a certain level. People will rise to that level, rise to whatever challenge is necessary to fulfill their obligations, but sometimes they just need to be reminded of those expectations. It was this dedicated consciousness-raising that led to a more cohesive and transparent way of governance for Volunteers of America."*

Representation from the local affiliate brings tremendous value to the organization, such as a deeper understanding of internal issues and organizational culture and how that understanding can contribute to the decision-making process. But at times this led to a category of board members who believed or acted as if they had insider or superior information (the "insider"). The troublesome behaviors that sometimes arose as a result were that both the outsiders and insiders concluded that the suggestions or insights offered by the insiders in meetings were somehow more meaningful. These insiders traded knowledge through sidebars and offline meetings, sometimes leaving others with innuendo that compromised board decisions. The outsiders sometimes felt left out.

When Chuck became the chief executive, he and the board chair, Frances Hesselbein, addressed this issue in a series of open and candid discussions between them. They then expanded the dialogue to include the executive committee, and eventually brought it to the full board at a board retreat.

The resulting discussion confirmed that the organization had a need for

- consistent transparency
- specific information or data upon which a decision was based to be made available to all in advance
- everyone involved to have a solid understanding of the question at hand
- all discussions to take place in a full group setting within official meetings

It was also candidly discussed that insiders serving on the national board must take off their "local" hat and look at the larger perspective, making decisions that were in the best interests of the organization as a whole and not basing their vote on how the decision was likely to impact their individual affiliate organization. Finally, it was confirmed that decision making would be a shared process. Once the consensus decision was made, it was publicly supported as a decision of the organization.

## FAILURE TO MANAGE PERSONAL ISSUES OR SPECIAL CASES

One of the keys to managing a troublesome board member with logical action instead of illogical reaction is labeling the behavior rather than the individual, and dealing with each case directly and in a timely manner. When patterns of chronic behavior exhibit themselves, these could be personal elements that may or may not be fixable. If they are completely ignored, or if too much time passes before others face up to the fact that the behaviors are challenging the overall work of the board, it may be too late to avoid personal resentment and damaged morale. One troublesome behavior, especially if not addressed, might lead to other troublesome behaviors from the same individual, and could even provoke troublesome behaviors in others where none existed before.

Martial arts instructors teach not to pull away from an attacker but to join the attacker. If the victim flows with the attacker's direction and energy, it can turn to the victim's benefit. For example, if the person under attack attempts to pull away from a stranglehold from behind, he risks breaking his neck. Instead, if he pushes backward in the direction in which the assailant is pulling, he will cause the attacker to lose footing and grip. Too often, the troublesome board member is opposed or ignored, and others pull away or turn their backs. That resistance creates a tug-of-war and establishes an adversarial relationship that goes nowhere. Going with the resistance requires staying close to troublesome board members instead of isolating them, as painful as that tactic may seem. Opportunities for ongoing contact and conversation should be provided so the board member can be heard.[6]

Further discussion of intervention takes place within the analysis and recommendations in Chapters 2, 3, and 4. It is important to note, however, that these conversations are usually led by the board chair alone, or the chair along with the governance committee or executive committee. Or, given the nature of the behavior, a separate task force might even be established or a trained facilitator brought in to resolve the conflict. A specific meeting (time and place) should be designated for this purpose. Those delegated to lead the conversation should meet in advance to settle on how to approach the individual, who will say what, and what specific outcomes they hope to achieve from the conversation. As with any feedback, the meeting will have the greatest impact if the tone is positive, polite, and reflects expected productivity. (See Necessary Knowledge: Giving and Receiving Feedback, on page 16.)

6. Adapted from Bailey, Mark. *The Troublesome Board Member*. Washington, DC: BoardSource (formerly the National Center for Nonprofit Boards), 1996. Page 11.

## Necessary Knowledge

### No Two Boards Are Alike

The first step to board service is to reduce the many ambiguities that inevitably accompany it. However, the following realities must not be overlooked:

- No generic model of board size, composition, or structure has proven itself viable to all circumstances. On the other hand, a body of knowledge has evolved that argues for certain structures, policies, and practices that consistently work better than others.

- All organizations undergo a metamorphosis that calls for periodic evaluation, fine-tuning, and sometimes major overhaul of their governance structures. Organizational performance, like human performance, is cyclical in effectiveness and needs renewal as it evolves over time.

- Boards and board members perform best when they exercise their responsibilities primarily by asking good, timely questions rather than by managing programs or implementing their own policies. The relationship between the board and the staff tends to be strongest when expectations are mutual and responsibilities are clear.[7]

---

7. Ingram, Richard T. *Ten Basic Responsibilities of Nonprofit Boards*. Washington, DC: BoardSource, 2003. Page viii.

# *Chapter 2: Poor Boardsmanship*

As already discussed (and hopefully understood even before opening the pages of this book) there are certain expectations regarding individual board members' conduct and responsibilities in fulfilling board activities. These can be specifically documented legal expectations, or simply those that come with the general understanding of the boardroom as a professional setting. Most of all, these expectations come with each and every board member's commitment to govern an organization. Although some troublesome behaviors may be overlapping, those categorized here as poor boardsmanship tend to carry more serious organizational consequences.

The behaviors discussed below stem from a variety of issues and result in related and many times similar impacts, but the discussion is framed around 1) general board member laziness that affects meeting efficiency, 2) the individual board member's lack of respect for the collective board process, 3) lack of clarity regarding board culture, and 4) the inevitable challenge of duality of interests when serving on a board. Each discussion defines a specific behavior, describes the impact on the full board or individual board members, includes a case study to illustrate and analyze the behavior, and then provides solutions for dealing with the behavior. Because these cases are largely based on real-life examples, it is important to note that some cases may illustrate more than one troublesome behavior. For the purposes of discussion, the author acknowledges this and asks the reader to extract the learning appropriately.

## DISRUPTED BOARD MEETINGS

The following behaviors are tied to general apathy of an individual board member. When board members ignore the minimum requirements of board service it is most likely caused by irresponsibility rather than a misunderstanding or a personal conflict. In the cases that follow, some or all of these measures could be taken to prevent the behavior from forming:

- Identify and manage *expectations* of board members — verbally during the recruitment phase, on paper during orientation, and with additional verbal reminders during onboarding.

- Make *requirements* absolutely clear on a regular basis (in addition to the initial orientation).

- Always hold all board members accountable for their actions.

- Institute documented recourse for failures to fulfill board obligations, such as removal policies or mechanisms; be sure they are distributed, reviewed, and approved by the full board.

- Apply any necessary recourse in a consistent manner so that all board members understand the consequences of irresponsible behavior.

## Necessary Knowledge

### Giving and Receiving Feedback

After-the-fact conversation starters have been provided for some of the case studies in Chapters 2 and 3. Most often, the first step in managing a troublesome board member is to initiate that conversation. By meeting with the board member, the board chair and/or responsible committee can clarify perceptions, develop options for resolution, solicit the board member's understanding and agreement to a course of action, and plan for follow-up afterwards to ensure a successful resolution for all.

Giving and receiving feedback takes conscious effort and can be most successful if those involved understand that some simple ground rules will make all the difference in the world.

**When *giving* feedback:**

- Ask if you can give feedback and if it's the right time. Honor the answer.

- State your intention as to why you wish to give feedback.

- Ask if the person has any questions or responses and then *listen.*

- Set up a future time to continue the discussion if necessary.

- Respect the person for hearing you out.

- Thank the person for listening.

How do you say something that should be obvious without letting the board member think he or she is being insulted?

- Be descriptive rather than evaluative. By repeating what you understood the other person to say without evaluating the content, the speaker is reassured that he or she is being listened to and understood.

- Be specific. By citing examples of specific behavior, the individual will better understand how he or she acted inappropriately and how to avoid the situation in the future.

- Focus on the feelings of the person who has experienced the behavior and is offering the feedback. By using the "I" language rather than making accusations about the other person, the person giving feedback prevents automatic, defensive responses and increases the likelihood that his or her point will be considered. It is difficult to challenge a statement about how someone feels.

- Direct the conversation at elements of the behavior the receiver can do something about. Only feedback that has the potential to solicit a change in behavior is constructive.

- Time it well. Feedback can be ineffective if tempers are too high or the current situation has degenerated beyond salvage. Time your feedback so that it is given when it is least threatening.

- Check to ensure clear communication. Ending feedback with a summation of the conversation ensures that you have made your point clearly and that the individual understands how his or her behavior affects the group.

- Avoid "dumping" or "unloading" on the other person. Feedback is not a venting process; it is designed to help the individual make positive changes in his or her behavior. Feedback used to "get something off your chest" is rarely effective and may alienate the recipient.

- Don't ask "Why?" It is not effective to ask someone why they act in a certain way — often, they won't know. It is better to focus on the future and how the behavior can be improved.[8]

**When *receiving* feedback:**

- Be sure you are in the right frame of mind to hear what's being offered. If not, set another time that would be better.

- Listen (active listening) and breathe deeply to keep yourself calm and focused.

- Respect the other person for offering the feedback.

- Ask clarifying questions to increase your understanding of what is being offered.

- Resist the impulse to defend at this time. Take time to think about what you've heard.

- Don't disagree — there may be an ounce of truth that you must consider before responding.

- Schedule a time to reconvene and finish the discussion.

- Thank the person for giving the feedback.

Ultimately, of course, learning from the conversation and deriving preventative strategies can reduce the risk of similar situations in the future.

---

8. Bailey, Mark. *The Troublesome Board Member*. Washington, DC: BoardSource (formerly the National Center for Nonprofit Boards), 1996. Page 11.

Some of the behaviors below suggest more specific preemptive solutions, and all will require additional action. Keep the list on page 15 in mind as you read the specific cases and their solution strategies.

## BEHAVIOR: DOESN'T COME TO MEETINGS

**Definition:** When a board member is consistently absent at board meetings and other organizational events in which he or she is expected to attend and participate in some way.

**Impact:** This behavior is troublesome when it is chronic. When expected or required input is compromised due to absence, other board members find themselves having to cover for the absent board member or doing his or her expected work. It may become irritating to the point where the other board members, in meetings when the board member is present, no longer "hear" his or her input because it is either not relevant or they feel it is not dependable. This behavior may also allow other board members to think it is acceptable to skip future events or meetings themselves. Additionally, by not fulfilling the duty of care — failing to exercise reasonable care while making a decision as a steward of the organization (not participating in the decision-making process) — a board member places liability risks on himself or herself.

**Case:** *Jeff Jones joined the board of the Save the Birds of the Pacific organization last June. It is now April and Jeff has attended only one meeting. Everyone thought having Jeff on the board would be so great. He owns a yacht in the harbor and last November hosted a wonderful sunset cruise for our large donors. We really don't want to lose Jeff, but other board members are starting to grumble: "We make it a point to be at every board meeting, why doesn't he?"*

### Solution Strategy: Now What?

Before a person accepts an invitation to serve on a board, his number one obligation is to understand the board meeting schedule and accept the invitation only if he can commit to attending meetings. Ideally, the board meeting calendar is set at least one year in advance, with all board members having the opportunity to discuss the best date and time for everyone.

When board members are absent from the process of discussion and brainstorming, it automatically pushes the team backwards toward an earlier, more formative stage of development. Absence endangers a member's capacity to both be educated and to inform others, and it compromises quorum. A quorum — which defines how many board members must be in the room before a meeting can begin — should exist and be followed. It ensures that one or just a few board members do not make decisions without the board's consent. Many state laws set a quorum as a majority of voting board members if the bylaws do not define other standards. Quorum should, however, be included in the bylaws. A review of the bylaws will remind board members why their presence is essential.

Occasional board member absence from meetings is a fact of life, but it does not or should not happen often. All board members should be aware of the only acceptable reasons to be absent — illness, a death in the family, or other extreme personal or professional issues. In these cases, unless it is virtually impossible to do so, the board chair should be notified of absences in advance. When absence is occasional, the board has a responsibility to keep the absent board member up to speed. A good practice is to make notes of the meeting discussions to be provided to board members who are not present, along with a follow-up from a member of the governance committee. This will ensure that absent board member(s) have reviewed the discussion and have the opportunity to ask questions or provide additional comments at the next meeting. It will save the group unnecessary time and energy in updating absent members during the next meeting, also preventing other troublesome behaviors from forming due to lack of information or a misunderstanding.

If the absence is chronic — in the case of either acceptable or unacceptable excuses — the behavior must be dealt with directly. Either the board chair or the governance committee chair is responsible for dealing with the issue (and this person should know of his or her responsibility ahead of time). The responsible party should speak directly and assertively with the board member in question and restate the expectation about board meeting attendance. It is helpful to dig deep enough to understand the reasons for the board member's absence in order to choose the best approach for conversation. If it is unclear what the real problem is, there is a possibility the board member may be losing interest in the board's work. He may be dodging a problem or misunderstanding with a fellow board member. Or, the chronic absences may be a way of sending the message, "I want out!" The first step of intervention will make it easier to come up with options for what should happen next, even if the individual is ultimately asked to step down.

### After-the-Fact Conversation Starter

**Board chair or governance committee chair:** *"Jeff, your input is so incredibly necessary to the board's work. We really need you at our meetings. Your absence has created problems for us. May we count on you to regularly attend future meetings?*

*"I believe that we covered our meeting schedule when we first met with you about coming onto the board and you did not mention that this would be a problem. Perhaps we have scheduled our meetings at a time when you just can't make it. Is this the problem? Should we see if there is another time that works better for you and still works for the others? I'm not sure this is possible — it may be difficult to get the other 11 of us to rearrange our schedules at this point in time — but I would be willing to at least raise the issue.*

*"If you can't make the commitment to attend, I know you will understand that we will have to replace you with someone who can and we will accept your resignation."*

Having a direct conversation with the board member about this issue will remind him of the agreement to live up to the expectation of attending meetings. Again, it may also ferret out another issue contributing to his absence, or that the board member's commitment to the organization has changed due to other things in his personal life.

## Behavior: Arrives Late to Meetings

**Definition:** When a board member is consistently late to board meetings and/or other organizational events in which he or she is expected to attend and participate in some way.

**Impact:** When expected or required participation is compromised due to lateness, other board members sometimes find themselves having to cover for the absent board member or doing his or her expected work. This behavior either causes the entire group to wait on the missing board member's arrival or it eventually interrupts the flow of the meeting, requiring the group to provide recaps so that the individual can be engaged in the rest of the conversation. Regardless, it wastes the precious time of everyone involved, taking away from the focus of the discussions and many times causing the meeting to end later than planned. The tardy board member misses key parts of the discussion, affecting his or her ability to contribute to the rest of the meeting and affecting the quorum if there are votes taking place. This behavior may also allow other board members to think it acceptable to neglect the determined start time at future events or meetings themselves.

**Case:** *Ever since she joined the board, Sue Smart has attended every board meeting, as well as her assigned committee meetings. But she is perpetually 20 to 30 minutes late to each one. She apologizes profusely as she blows in, but then there's usually a minimum of five minutes of others saying, "Oh it's OK, we understand, traffic is so difficult this time of day," etc. But privately, board members are talking offline, saying they are getting sick of accommodating Sue. I'm afraid someone is really going to blow up at her one of these days!*

### Solution Strategy: Now What?

Occasional board member tardiness at meetings is also a fact of life. Grumbling or complaining about it is wasted energy. But, being on time is expected — not just because it should be an understood obligation, but simply out of basic politeness and respect for everyone else's time. If the tardiness is occasional, the board member has a responsibility to get herself up to speed. If she knows in advance that she will be late, a board member should

- let the board chair or another officer or member know that she will be late so that the meeting can go ahead and start without her

- refrain from commenting on business completed or in discussion prior to her arrival so that the team can move forward with the participants who have all the information

- follow up soon after the meeting or during a break with another board member to see what she missed

This will save the group unnecessary time and energy in having to repeat everything for the tardy board member during the meeting. In the case above, the board has no formal responsibility to interrupt the meeting and inform her of what she has already missed. The board chair can explain this gently, telling the tardy board member that she will be "filled in" after the meeting.

If the tardiness is chronic, something must be done to deal with it directly. Active participation should be considered obligatory. Asking questions, providing feedback, sharing ideas, or refusing to accept easy solutions all contribute to the needed base for wise decision making. And when a board member arrives in the middle of it all, she misses key points of discussion, finding it impossible to be an active participant. Either the board chair or the governance committee chair needs to intervene and restate the expectation about being on time for board meetings. If it is unclear what the real problem is, there is a possibility the board member may be losing interest in the board's work.

For the good of the entire board process, the board chair may wish to explore or lead a discussion about meetings in general:

- Are meetings boring, badly prepared, or poorly chaired?

- Are all the various meetings necessary?

- Are unimportant issues or "old business" first on the agenda?

- Are meetings too long, held at an inconvenient time, or not scheduled enough in advance?

- Is the location of various meetings inconvenient?

### After-the-Fact Conversation Starter

**Board chair:** *"Sue, you are so incredibly busy. We deeply appreciate that you have committed yourself to this organization by being on our board. But we need to find a way to make sure you are with us at the start of each meeting so you don't miss out on important information that might frame the discussion for the rest of the meeting, harming your ability to participate. How can we help you? Do we need to consider changing our start times? (Using humor) We could always tell you that the meeting is starting a half-hour earlier than it actually does!"*

*"I'm not sure that I can get all other nine of us to agree to start 30 minutes later. But maybe we could compromise at 15 minutes later if you can commit to us that you will be on time."*

### BEHAVIOR: COMES UNPREPARED

**Definition:** When a board member consistently comes to meetings without having read the agenda or other distributed materials ahead of time, and having failed to do any assigned research or reporting to provide information, insight, or input on a particular subject for the rest of the board.

**Impact:** Having to bring someone up to date in meetings that were specifically designated for discussion and consensus based on previously provided information slows down the rest of the board and may prevent the necessary decision making from happening at the meeting as planned. The discussion can only move forward efficiently with the careful deliberation of all board members. If someone comes unprepared, the process is flawed and wasteful. When a board member participates without the necessary background knowledge the board may ultimately "turn off" the voice of the individual due to lack of confidence in his or her ability to make a fully informed decision.

**Case:** *Peter Porter comes to meetings but hasn't read a single thing in advance! The board committees and staff faithfully pull together pertinent reports to send out at least a week ahead of time so that we can come with questions or suggestions — especially concerning the finance committee's report — but Peter never does his homework. It wouldn't be so bad, I guess, if not for the fact that Peter then insists on asking time-consuming questions about things that are clearly spelled out. It's almost as if he wants to prove he's contributing by speaking up. But if he would just read the documents, we could use the time in the meetings for other necessary and valuable discussion.*

## What Could Have Been Done?

In this case, was the material distributed to all board members with enough time to adequately review and prepare for the meeting (two weeks before a meeting is usually recommended)?

## Solution Strategy: Now What?

If there is a single failure (or on very rare occasion) to do the homework, then the board member has an obligation to refrain from commenting in a discussion where he or she may not have the full information to do so. Board members can agree in advance that this will be part of the team process so it is expected each time. If it is stated as part of a meeting's standard operating procedure, the board chair is responsible for setting the standards and managing this process.

When poor preparedness happens often and questions arise as a result, the board chair could gently illustrate the point to the board member by citing the homework materials (with the answers) during meeting time. Regardless, the chair should meet with the board member in question after the meeting to discuss his behavior and how it is affecting the group process. Ask the board member what information he might find helpful. Is he receiving enough? Too much? What format is best in order to digest it appropriately? Additionally, using this topic with the entire group as a subject for ongoing board development on an annual basis may prevent this troublesome behavior. Not only will it surface any concerns or areas for improvement so that the process can be revised on a regular basis, but it will cultivate an aspect of organizational culture that meeting attendees will come fully prepared as an indication of respect for everyone else's time.

## After-the-Fact Conversation Starter

**Board chair:** (Coaching) *"Peter, I need your help. We need to make our meetings more efficient and effective — we need to make sure that we dedicate our limited time together to clarifying questions and a deeper discussion of our options. Can I ask you to model this in the next meeting by coming with two or three questions that specifically relate to the information we are receiving in advance of the meeting? Or, how about I call you the morning of the meeting so we can go over the considerations we need to pose to the group?"*

(Intervention) *"Peter, your comments and suggestions at our board meetings are very insightful. But, it has become clear over the course of several meetings that you do not take the time to review the information packages prior to the meeting. I need to ask you to start doing this on a regular basis. We are getting bogged down in rehashing the information that was already shared instead of moving into the decision-making process. Can I count on you to come to the meetings prepared so that we can move forward in a more effective and productive way?"*

---

## FOOD FOR THOUGHT

*"Shame on our organizations if we don't vet our nominees well enough to avoid troublesome board member calamity. We reap what we sow when we rush the nomination process, take someone's best friend without first-hand experience, or give in to the one-shot generous by awarding her a seat instead of a plaque. But take heart, even the worst are redeemable if the rest of the board does not capitulate in the face of its duty to provide ethical and responsible corporate oversight through majority rules. There is little a board member can do of ill that a sensible board majority cannot fix with a little peer pressure, some confident and clear leadership, and, if need be, enforceable term limits. But if the majority fails, the board deserves its fate."*

Eliot Pfanstiehl, President/CEO, Strathmore Hall Foundation, Inc., North Bethesda, MD

*"I feel it is absolute and imperative to have term limits and board rotation. It's hard to recruit good people to serve on a board if they think there's no end in sight! And it is in the organization's best interests to bring on new blood on a regular basis. I see an energy arch with regard to board service. The first couple of years a person is on a board should be about learning and getting involved. The third, fourth, or fifth years should be spent in leadership positions to truly give your all. The last few years are about being an 'elder statesmen' and providing the benefit of the history and depth of knowledge from your years of service before you might burn out on that organization. If you think of it this way, then 6–8 years is a pretty effective run for both the board member and the organization."*

Richard W. Snowdon III, The Hill-Snowdon Foundation, Washington, DC

---

## WEAKENED PERSONALITY OF THE BOARD

The following behaviors are tied to ignorance or lack of clarity regarding "the way of the board." Every board is different and all boards face occasional change in membership, structure, and focus. When board members are unsure or uninformed regarding board culture, the entire group needs to take a step back to get everyone on the same page. In the cases that follow, some or all of these measures could be taken to prevent the behavior from forming:

- Hold an annual retreat apart from traditional board meetings to focus on process and strategy.

- Provide continuous board development to ensure that mission, vision, and values are embedded in board work.

- As a team, revisit the board structure, including committees and the nature of their assignments, to be sure work is being done in the most efficient way and with a common understanding.

- Be sure all board members understand the expectations and limitations of board-staff relationships.

- Create job descriptions for the board as a whole, individual board members, board officers, and committees so there are no misunderstandings regarding specific roles and responsibilities.

- Always, always, always do the proper recruitment, orientation, and onboarding, regardless of the unique reasons or circumstances around someone's invitation to join the board. Not only does this prevent the board from bringing new people on for the wrong reasons, but it is also beneficial for prospective board members to engage in a detailed learning phase in which the organizational history, culture, and process is made clear so the board members can be sure that the organization is a good match for them too.

- Be sure term limits are enforced. It should be a regular process for the governance committee to re-review each board member before reelection so that no one is surprised or insulted when the time comes.

- Consider trial periods for incoming board members. This is a good way of gauging whether or not someone is the right fit. Some boards allow board candidates a seat on a committee or task force before actually joining the board, testing the waters for the board and for the candidates themselves.

Some of the following behaviors suggest more specific preemptive solutions and all will require additional action. Keep the list above in mind as you read the specific cases and their solution strategies.

---

## FOOD FOR THOUGHT

*"Arena Stage in Washington, DC, uses a model that I like. All board members are initially brought on for a one-year term. It gives both the board member and the institution a chance to see if it's a good fit. Usually you can tell within the first six months if it is or it isn't. Near the end of the first year, the board chair and the board member sit down and talk about how it's going. If they mutually agree, then the board member is nominated for a three-year term, which could then be renewed for an additional three-year term. If a board member serves two full three-year terms, then he or she must stand down for at least a year before being nominated to serve again. Usually good board members are kept 'onboard' as active volunteers for that year and then can be renominated for regular board service for another stint. It's a great model that has served Arena really well."*

Richard W. Snowdon III, The Hill-Snowdon Foundation, Washington, DC

## Behavior: Confuses Roles and Responsibilities

**Definition:** When a board member either naively or consciously fails to fulfill his or her stated responsibilities as a board member, confusing the board member role with that of the board chair, the chief executive, or other members of the staff.

**Impact:** This behavior makes it difficult for others to get their jobs done efficiently. It takes the board backward in having to redefine roles and responsibilities, and can even lead to attempted micromanagement of board or organizational operations and inappropriate interactions with other individuals involved (whether board members or staff). Inappropriate interactions with colleagues can cause poor internal communication, a decrease in productivity, and low morale.

**Case:** *Bob Barnes was excited to be part of the leadership of a nonprofit that was largely staff-driven and used its volunteer board for brainstorming and external strategic contacts for fundraising purposes. He had not been the most active board member, but he was sincere and he always did what he said he would do. He was recommended for a board officer position and was confident that he could do the job well, vowing to recommit himself to the organization.*

*Margaret Manning started out with the organization as an administrative assistant. After two years, a manager position opened and because the organization committed to hiring from within when possible, the senior staff agreed that they should give Margaret a chance. She had done very well as an administrative assistant. Unfortunately, it became clear that Margaret was having a very hard time making the transition to management. In her new position, she had several peer relationships to manage and her work required successful interactions with other departments to perform services and meet deadlines. When she failed to meet a deadline, she would blame others. Each time Margaret disagreed with a decision, she openly complained. She was often critical of other employees and of her supervisor when things did not go her way.*

*When Margaret began to suspect that her position at the organization might be in jeopardy, she called on Bob to air her "grievances." Bob was quite concerned. The way Margaret characterized it made it look like she was being harassed unfairly by the other employees and by her supervisor. He called the chief executive, Elizabeth Eckard.*

**Bob:** (After some small talk) *"Elizabeth, I actually wanted to talk to you about a staff morale problem I've been hearing about."*

**Elizabeth:** *"My goodness, Bob. I'm surprised to hear that there is any problem and I'm especially surprised to be hearing about it from you."*

**Bob:** *"It seems like some of your staff are unfairly criticizing other staff members' work. I'm not going to name names, but maybe you should call an all-staff meeting and get things out in the open."*

*Elizabeth made a few discreet inquiries. She trusted her senior staff and did not want to make any waves where there were none. She knew if there was something really serious happening with her staff it would be brought to her attention.*

*About a week later, Bob called again.*

**Bob:** *"Elizabeth, I'm sorry to tell you this, but this situation seems to be getting worse."*

**Elizabeth:** *"I've done some investigating, Bob, and quite frankly, I don't have a clue as to what the 'situation' is. You're going to have to give me some specifics."*

*And he did. He gave Elizabeth a litany of complaints that Margaret had made to him over the past few months.*

*Elizabeth met with Margaret's supervisor, Alicia. Alicia told Elizabeth that Margaret was having performance issues and that Alicia and the HR director had more than a few counseling sessions with her. She gave more details, making it obvious that these meetings hadn't gone well and seemed to only be making things worse.*

*Elizabeth called Bob back and told him that the situation was more complicated than he had been led to understand, but that she would stay on top of it. She thanked him for bringing it to her attention. But it didn't end there for Bob. Over the course of the next few days, Margaret would call Bob, who would then call Elizabeth. At first, Elizabeth did her best to tell Bob that it was all under control. Then, based on something Bob said about perhaps promoting Margaret even further to relieve the tension, Elizabeth had to tell Bob he was interfering with management issues.*

*The situation escalated. Bob began calling other board members and complaining that the chief executive was allowing harassment within the organization. The other board members individually called Elizabeth, who explained calmly and rationally the history of the situation and that she felt Bob's view of his role as the champion of this employee was simply not appropriate board member behavior.*

*A few other board members tried to intervene. They met with Bob and privately indicated that neither his role as a board officer nor the role of any board member included this kind of intervention with regard to internal operational issues, but there was no change in Bob's behavior. He asked for a meeting of the executive committee. At that meeting he put forth a motion to terminate the chief executive. The executive committee members informed Bob that his motion would not be seconded. They also told him that his involvement in the situation was inappropriate and that his behavior toward the chief executive undermined her position.*

## Solution Strategy: Now What?

A member of the board heard something of concern, made a call to the chief executive, and was told that it would be looked into and taken care of. That should have ended it unless further hard evidence came up that led to a suspicion of illegality, financial impropriety, or unethical behavior. Board members have a responsibility to support the chief executive in his or her delegated authority to run the day-to-day management of the organization. If the full board concludes that the chief executive has violated the board's trust in any way, it should follow protocol for the evaluation and, if necessary, removal of the chief executive. Anything other than that is not the role of the board. Additionally, it is inappropriate under most circumstances for board members to have direct communication with staff members other than the chief executive about organizational issues and operations or without the chief executive's prior approval. Both the board and the entire staff should have the understanding that any and all communication to the board must go through the chief executive.

The board chair needs to have a serious face-to-face conversation with Bob to be sure he truly understands why the other board members disagree with his behavior and why the executive committee denied his motion. The board chair needs to remind Bob of his individual responsibilities as a board officer and a member of the entire group, clarifying the differences in board roles and the role of the chief executive in situations like this. Then, the board chair and Bob need to come to an agreement regarding the options for the future of Bob's board service. If he can't let this one go, he may need to leave his board seat altogether.

## BEHAVIOR: MICROMANAGES

**Definition:** When a board member — whether it's the chair or a member who does not hold an officer position — inappropriately "overmanages" the rest of the group, monitoring the work of others too closely, stepping in to another person's job function when it is unwarranted, and operating independently rather than through the group.

**Impact:** Micromanagement can be confusing and exhausting for everyone. It is at best duplication of effort and at worst demotivating by not allowing others to do their own job. The board member who is micromanaging fails to do his or her work effectively because the focus is on the work of others. It is not uncommon for things to fall between the cracks, and resentment fills the space. Ultimately, an "overengaged" board member leads to the disengagement of other members (board or staff) and processes begin to break down, discussions lose meaning, and the team effort is lost.

**Case:** *Brad Bentley hit it big. Brad's little basement idea turned into a monster business overnight. The big guns swooped in and now Brad is a multimillionaire "retiree" at age 37.*

*Brad's neighbor, Lori, asked Brad to come with her to a benefit dinner. Lori served on the board of a human services organization in Brad's community and the benefit was being held to raise funds for that organization. Brad had never heard of the organization before, but at the dinner he met members of the community who had been well served by the organization, as well as the chief executive and other board members, and was very impressed.*

*The next morning, Brad called the chief executive, Richard, and told him he wanted to serve on the board. Richard explained to Brad that the board had a process for bringing on new members, but that he was delighted to hear of Brad's interest.*

*Lori and Richard were both thrilled. They knew that Brad had millions, but Lori also shared with Richard that Brad was somewhat flighty. She said, "We need to strike while the iron is hot or I think we'll lose him to another organization." Lori and Richard split up the board list and started making calls that day. Brad visited the office and met the staff. He looked over all the materials. Richard told him about their programs. The board had been canvassed and they agreed to bring Brad onto the board immediately.*

*Brad came to his first meeting a week later and made a splash. When he was introduced, he thanked everyone for bringing him on the board and he promptly gave Richard a check for the organization in the amount of $25,000. But at that first meeting came the first signs of trouble. The third agenda item concerned the discussion of a possible new building for increased services in another area of the community. Brad jumped right into the* discussion, arguing against the proposed location and pushing for another one. He felt strongly that his proposed location was "up and coming" and that the building would make a great investment for the group. The other board members were a little taken aback by Brad's very strong opinion at his very first meeting. They knew that he must have been a little confused about the purpose of such a building — that it was for services to the population there in the proposed community, not as an investment for the organization. But Brad was excited; he offered to go look at buildings in the area he was recommending and said he would get back to the board with a report. No one wanted to challenge him at his very first meeting and they agreed that he should go ahead. It was nice that he wanted to get so involved right away.

Brad went charging ahead. He met with real estate developers and actively started negotiating deals on behalf of the organization. In the end, the building he thought would be the best investment actually cost $100,000 more than the one the board committee had originally proposed after months of research. But Brad was still convinced, and presented a purchase agreement to the board at the next meeting. He said they needed to sign it right away and that the investment return on "his" building would be four times that of the other one. The board tabled the decision, but Brad assumed it was a "go."

In this case, and in others that rapidly followed, Brad began to actively clash with the other board members. He also started ordering the staff to follow up on a variety of ideas and initiatives that he thought should be done on an almost weekly basis.

## What Could Have Been Done?

Lori's acknowledgment of Brad's "flighty" tendencies should have sparked further questioning from the board leaders and taken as a sign that he may move on to new things without careful consideration.

## Solution Strategy: Now What?

New board members owe it to themselves and to the rest of the board to get to know not only what has happened and what is happening with the organization, but also who the players are and how they interact. The first few meetings should be used to develop a full understanding of what the organization has already accomplished, the current strategic issues it is facing, the group dynamics, relationships and personal styles of the other board members, and the level of work and participation that is expected.

In a perfect world, a mature organization would rarely bring on a board member who had not served on a nonprofit board before. Organizations that are no longer in the startup phase of organizational development need experienced board members who are capable of looking at issues from all angles and making hard, strategic decisions. If there was a rush in bringing on a new member and the board can't turn back now, the board chair might try implementing a buddy system to give the new board member a deeper understanding of organizational mission, history, culture, and basic board responsibilities.

Additionally, it is the board chair's responsibility to intervene and ask the governance committee to go back and do an orientation "after the fact" with Brad, defining the roles and responsibilities of the board as a working body, and of board members as individuals. Providing the board member with written resources, as well as offering the opportunity to participate in workshops or other trainings to increase his understanding of the new role, could help.

In some extreme cases, such as the one illustrated above, dealing with the situation after the fact may be very difficult. The conversation is not going to be easy and it may be that the new board member just won't get it. But for the long-term good of the organization, a discussion about the troublesome behavior would be a positive next step. And, in the end, the board will be wiser after coming to terms with the situation.

## BEHAVIOR: FAILS TO INTEGRATE INTO ORGANIZATIONAL CULTURE

**Definition:** Organizational culture can be defined as a relatively unstated, undefined set of beliefs, knowledge, attitudes, and/or traditions that operate as subtext under an organization's formal structure and operations. Culture may exhibit itself as negative or positive. It may be actively promoted or indirectly followed. When a board member has a set of beliefs, knowledge, attitudes, or traditions that are at odds with those generally accepted and applied within an organization, conflict is often the result. This frequently manifests itself when a new board member sees himself or herself as a self-appointed change agent.

**Impact:** Failure to integrate into the established organizational culture can be a confusing and frustrating experience for the board member because he or she may not understand that this is the actual cause of those feelings. Or, when a board member who strongly believes that somehow the "old way of doing things" is wrong and it is up to him or her to make a change, other board members may be influenced by the change agent, causing factions or cliques and breaking apart the communication and teamwork ethic.

**Case:** *Rona Ramsey always described herself as a "Type-A" personality. She climbed to the top of the corporate ladder faster than most and now headed up the mergers and acquisitions department of a major company. She heard from one of her colleagues that The Dance Theatre was actively looking for more corporate representation and so she approached the organization and offered to serve on their board. The current board was made up mostly of other artists, patrons, and a few artistic academics, many of whom had served for a long, long time. While things were going well, they did think that maybe having more diversity of experience on their board might bring in new patrons and clients.*

*The Dance Theatre did great work and had an excellent reputation in the community. It had been around for 15 years and the current artistic director, Seria Sloane, was its founder. While The Dance Theatre did not have many resources — financial or human — at its disposal, it was a thriving organization with a lot of laughter, fun, and good will. Much of the backstage and administrative support was gladly done pro bono by volunteers. They made ends meet and were relatively content with the way things were.*

*Rona was interviewed and vetted and everyone agreed that she would make a great addition to the board. At her first meeting, Rona took a quick read of the financials and could see immediately that the best course of action would be for The Dance Theatre to merge with another organization. If it did this, then the two organizations could share personnel and infrastructure, creating an economy of scale.*

*Over the next few months, Rona dug deep. She called staff members and pumped their brains without telling them why. She asked to see old financials and annual reports and put together a flowchart that demonstrated how organizational growth was sluggish and one year, at least on paper, actually went backwards. She prepared a business plan and researched a few other organizations that she thought would be compatible.*

*Members of the board and the staff knew that Rona was up to something, but they thought she was coming up with a great new plan to find more money or even to get them a better space.*

*At her second board meeting she came prepared to present her idea. When new business came up on the agenda, Rona asked to speak. Rona's idea came out of the blue for everyone else. Seria was extremely hurt and felt that maybe this was something the other board members had asked Rona to do without telling her — maybe they really did think it was time for The Dance Theatre to cease to exist and for her to step down. Some board members were extremely angry — how dare someone new just come in and decide that the organization should dismantle? Some of the other board members really didn't know what to think — Rona did have so much business experience. Maybe she was right...*

## What Could Have Been Done?

The board chair could have and should have stepped in as soon as she heard that Rona was questioning staff and eagerly seeking information from others. The board made a mistake by "waiting in eagerness to find out what Rona had to offer." The board chair should have been informed and could have prevented the shocking manner in which the merger was suggested.

By waiting a little longer and simply observing during her first few meetings, Rona could have gained a deeper understanding of the organization before making any suggestions for change, especially such a dramatic one.

## Solution Strategy: Now What?

The board chair should step in immediately and explain to the board member that her idea is too dramatic for serious consideration at this time — and why. However, the board could engage in some appreciative inquiry activities (using an acknowledgment of contribution and success rather than an analysis of dysfunction or failure) to create a common understanding of the organization in its current place. Since Rona put the idea of a merger on the table, the board could take the opportunity for a large-scale, big-idea brainstorming session, using it as a "devil's advocate" position. In addition to confirming what is working for the organization, such global dialogue could also surface some aspects for healthy and needed change that wouldn't have been considered otherwise.

## After-the-Fact Conversation Starter

**Board chair:** *"Hi, Rona. I wanted to follow up on your presentation at the board meeting last night. It's clear that you generated a mountain of research and analysis for us to consider. What I'd like to do is schedule a time at our retreat to talk about this, and pair the discussion with an exercise called appreciative inquiry. This would allow us to also look at what's working at all levels with The Dance Theatre. I think the result of this* discussion and a discussion of your proposal may get us to thinking about what actions, if any, we need to take.

*"In the meantime, though, I did want to talk to you about how some members of the board, including Seria, took your ideas. Given all the experience you have had, I'm hoping that you can help me find a way to help them understand that your ideas were offered in the spirit of trying to improve the organization rather than a criticism of how it is currently doing its business. I know it may not seem that we are the most effective or up-to-date organization that we could be, but for the most part, everyone has been pretty happy with what we have accomplished and we have a great time doing it. Can you help me think through how we can best do this?"*

This conversation may lead to

- Rona understanding that maybe she came on too strong, too soon

- Rona realizing that she is still on a learning curve and needs to gain a greater understanding of the organization and its culture

- Rona and the organization concluding that maybe this isn't the right place for her as a board member

- The organization understanding that it might be missing out on opportunities because it is staying in a comfort zone that could ultimately prevent growth or even long-term viability

## BEHAVIOR: DEVIATES FROM MISSION

**Definition:** When a board member's work strives for something other than the stated mission of the organization.

**Impact:** This behavior leads to wasted time and energy on everyone's part, and can cause loss of focus, commitment, and respect for the organization from other board members. In many cases, failure to understand mission leads to other troublesome behaviors in the same individual, such as bullying or not understanding roles.

**Case:** *Marcy Mettle came on the board early in the organization's recent growth period, invited in part because of her relative youth. The organization had been in existence for over 50 years. Formerly largely dependent on U.S. government grants, it grew fairly steadily for years, saw its revenues fall off somewhat over a period, and in the past five years has rapidly expanded its funding base to produce healthy surpluses. Also, in that period, the board's substantial representation of retired diplomatic and area experts were being supplemented by successful business people.*

*As she was recommended by one of the latter, Marcy was thought to have entrepreneurial experience and useful contacts in the region where most of the organization's activity occurred. However, it soon became obvious that her experience was very limited and her understanding of the organization and the role of a board minimal. Her contributions to meetings were largely irrelevant and, frankly, disrespectful of other board members and staff. Marcy specifically wanted the organization to become more political. She wanted the organization to be activist-oriented rather than service-oriented and became very* aggressive in meetings when the other board members and staff tried to explain to her why this couldn't be done.

As part of the organization's outreach, an international conference was planned. Marcy was asked to chair a panel featuring young people whose accomplishments had already been substantial and innovative. She insisted that the panel be used as a call for action and lobbying, which was clearly not what the organization did, or should do. She bullied the invited participants about this to such an extent that intervention was required and efforts to get things back on track were only partially successful. Not only had Marcy offended the invitees, but the board chair also had to engage in extended efforts to prevent Marcy from mistreating the staff.

As noted, the organization enjoyed a number of successful initiatives and expansions of existing operations, a record hard to criticize. However, Marcy failed to appreciate this and certainly tried to move the organization in this new direction by repeatedly proposing new programs and activities inconsistent with the organization's purpose and insisting on inappropriate board interference with day-to-day activities.

### Solution Strategy: Now What?

Marcy's failure to understand the organization's mission led to continual proposals inconsistent with the organization's intended work. In this specific case, the board chair's direct conversation with Marcy about lobbying and its consequences on the legal status of the organization would be in order. Quite often, there are other organizations that can lobby without limits on behalf of certain issues and Marcy could be directed to a lobbying organization with a similar mission. Her participation with an alternate lobbying or more politically oriented organization may be better suited for her interests.

All board members need training when coming on to a new board, no matter how experienced or inexperienced they may be. Each organization has a different mission with a different culture and a different way of doing things. In the future, the board may wish to minimize Marcy's impact by being very selective in giving her assignments. The board chair should make it a point to check up on her from time to time and use these conversations in an attempt to slowly get the right message across.

One way of reminding everyone why they're there is to make time for "mission moments" on every agenda for each board meeting. These mission moments take only five or 10 minutes of the group's time, and ask that each member shares with the rest of the group a recent experience he or she had that served as a reminder of why their work is so important to the community. It allows the board to take a step back as a group and remember the larger picture in the midst of the sometimes difficult issues. And, for those board members who haven't yet grasped the purpose of the organization, another education tactic may be better later than never.

Sometimes, the only way to resolve this sort of behavior is to wait until the board member's term limit is up and he or she can be rotated off the board.

# Pushing an "Uncollective" Board Process

The following behaviors are displayed when an individual disrespects the collective practices of the board. When board members fail to honor commitments to group process, it most likely stems from a misunderstanding of group norms and/or an inability or unwillingness to take part in shared responsibilities. In the cases that follow, some or all of these measures could be taken to prevent the behavior from forming:

- Always take meeting minutes and be sure assignments and individual commitments are given in writing and/or verbally in front of the group.

- Ensure an active governance committee that will communicate with board members and committees one-on-one to maintain the health of the board and an understanding of shared responsibility, as well as to hold all board members accountable.

- Require more active committee chairs who will follow up with individual committee members and gather the working group as a whole on a regular basis.

- A discussion on team theory and how decisions are reached and honored should take place during the orientation and onboarding process. Additionally, incoming board members should be educated on the board's background, culture, policies, and voting procedures.

- During recruitment and orientation it should be made absolutely clear that board members not only serve as public ambassadors for the organization, but also do their individual work on behalf of the entire group.

- Maintain a confidentiality policy and require all board members to review and sign it annually.

Some of the behaviors below suggest more specific preemptive solutions and all will require additional action. Keep the above in mind as you read the specific cases and their solution strategies.


## Behavior: Doesn't Follow Through

**Definition:** When a board member has been specifically tasked with a responsibility or activity and he or she fails to get it done.

**Impact:** Failure to complete an assigned task slows the forward movement of the board's work. It is frustrating to put an item on the agenda, carving time out of a meeting to discuss it, and then not have anything to discuss. It can have serious consequences if the task is deadline-oriented or prevents an aspect of time-sensitive planning or decision making from taking place. That being said, fellow board members will have a difficult time trusting the individual's work in the future, and may ultimately take on more work rather than risking setback and disappointment by trusting the individual with a new assignment.

**Case:** *We are trying to get more formalized in our board recruitment process. Alice Allen, one of our board members, used to serve on the board of Give Every Child a Computer.*

*Several board members have said they heard (and Alice confirmed) that the GECC board has a great recruitment process. Alice volunteered to contact someone on the board to ask if they would be willing to share their documents with our organization. Well, it has been four months now and Alice still hasn't done it. Her report is listed on every meeting agenda but she always seems to have one excuse or another for not having it. In the meantime, Bill Bonner has pulled together some other information about recruitment but he is reluctant to bring it up at a meeting because he doesn't want to hurt Alice's feelings. She got really touchy one time in the past when she thought she was being criticized and we just don't want to go through that again.*

**Solution Strategy: Now What?**

If it is clear that there is a pattern of behavior in this respect then at the very least the board could refrain from assigning the board member additional tasks in the

---

### FOOD FOR THOUGHT

Chicago community leader and leadership teacher Deborah A. Bricker tells the story of the breakthrough growth of The Goodman Theatre's board of directors that began about seven years ago. With a new building on the way and a corresponding increase in programs and operations, it became clear to Debbie and others that the board's members needed to increase their effectiveness and impact.

*"It started with a growing understanding on the part of some of the board members and staff that we were entering a new stage of organizational development. We just started working backwards in our discussions and said: This is what we are going to need — now what do we have to do to meet that need? We quickly began to realize that in order to meet the need, we were going to have to challenge our board, both individually and collectively, in a greater and more consistent way. And this started with a basic reclarification of board purpose."*

They formed a task force charged with clarifying trustee roles. The task force led six months of dialogue and discussion, collaboration, and consensus-building with all board members. They focused on two main areas: the service requirements of board members (full board responsibilities and committee responsibilities) and the financial requirements of board members (individual giving and fundraising). The result was a Trustees Responsibility Document and a process for implementing and holding board members accountable to the requirements of the document. The document was then voted on and approved by the full board.

*"Yes, there was some pushback. But what was valuable about the process is that we just kept moving forward until we got everyone to buy in. If someone didn't like something, we challenged him or her to come up with an alternative. It was give and take, back and forth. And the best thing was that the resulting document was group-created and approved."*

The process has been in place for some time now and is working effectively. Key elements include

- All board terms are for one year, renewable indefinitely based on the successful annual fulfillment of responsibilities.

---

future, even when she volunteers for such. One slip is enough to suggest that maybe another board member should perform a task along with her to help move the process along and get a better sense of what the problem might be. If that board member reports back that he or she did all the work without the reluctant board member's help, then this would be further feedback to use when talking to the individual about this behavior.

### After-the-Fact Conversation Starter

**Board chair:** *"Alice, I wanted to call you before the next meeting about your report. We need to move forward on revising the board recruitment process. I've also asked Bill to do some research into this and to provide some discussion points at the next meeting. Between his research and your report on the GECC process, we should be able to come to a*

---

*"We went to a one-year term with indefinite renewals because we thought that if someone cares enough about the theatre and wants to continue to work and to give to our mission, why should we rotate them off? This works for us."*

- Everyone is aware that all board members are being held to the same written expectations and that everyone around the table is still there because they have successfully met their obligations.

- At the beginning of the year, board members are asked to identify how they intend to fulfill their service and financial requirements in an easy-to-use reporting document.

- After nine months, the board nominating committee (with the staff support of the development department) provides a written progress report to each individual board member on how he or she has met the expectations.

- At the end of one year, board members receive another written progress report. If an individual board member has not met the obligations, a representative from the board nominating committee meets with the individual to find out why. If there are extenuating family, professional, or other understandable reasons, then the individual is asked if she feels she can fulfill her obligations in the coming year. If she says that she can, then the person is given a "by" and renominated for another term. If after a second year she still has not fulfilled her obligations, the board nominating committee accepts her resignation. There are no surprises for the individual, but the specific reasons for anyone's resignation are not shared with the whole.

*"It has worked. Our board has a $20,000 give or get, with a target of $40,000 per year. The average performance is usually in excess of $40,000. This is a terrific track record. But it only works because we constantly show our appreciation for our board members. I don't think there are many organizations that thank and recognize board members as much as we do. Being a volunteer board member is hard work. But for me, and I know for others on the board of The Goodman, the rewards are really worth it."*

*consensus for this next round of nominees. The governance committee has a deadline to submit the information, so time is of the essence. I think it would be a good idea for you and Bill to talk offline prior to the next meeting to make sure you won't be offering duplicate information. I'll have Bill give you a call."*

## BEHAVIOR: FAILS TO HONOR FINANCIAL COMMITMENTS

**Definition:** A reality that still eludes many individuals is that every board member has an obligation to contribute financially to the organization on an annual basis to the greatest extent possible, given his or her means.

**Impact:** Organizations will expect a certain amount of income from the annual financial contributions of the board. If one board member does not make his or her financial contribution, it may signal that the organization condones this in others and it could bend the behavior of the board as a whole. It also makes fundraising a challenging activity: Outside donors and funders will have a hard time giving their money if a board member can't say that he or she contributes to the cause. Additionally, when a board member promises a significant amount and then fails to give, other expense obligations of the organization become encumbered based on inaccurate receivables. Failure to make good on pledges made and accepted in good faith can have financial consequences, leading the organization to an unplanned deficit.

**Case:** *Dan Devine was the board chair of an exciting nonprofit. He joined the board when it was still a startup organization but became the board chair just as it was poised for a huge growth period. There was much discussion about the need to expand the board and bring on more diverse individuals to reflect the constituency. Another board member, Joe, came to Dan and told him that he had an excellent candidate for the board. Dan really respected his opinion and everyone in the community knew Joe, so if he said this board candidate would be good, Dan thought, "She must be!"*

*Charlene, the prospect, was invited to a few social events and what Dan and other board members found was a gregarious, open, and enthusiastic person who said all the right things. In fact, even before she was asked to be on the board, Charlene engaged the organization to play a significant role in a personal event she was organizing. In exchange, she said she would pay $25,000 for time and effort.*

*The event took place and was a huge success. Charlene came on the board shortly thereafter. When she was informed about the minimum personal contribution of board members in the amount of $1,000, Charlene smiled and said, "No problem! Just send me the bill!" Additionally, the organization was in the soft phase of a capital campaign and after the first presentation to the board, Charlene pulled Dan over and whispered in his ear, "Count on me for $30K."*

*Next on the horizon was the annual fundraising event. Each board member was expected to buy a ticket and attend, but was further encouraged to commit to a table, if possible, to help introduce new friends to the organization. At the meeting where the upcoming event was discussed, Charlene committed for two tables. Another $10,000!*

*The next day, Dan got a call from the chief executive and the development director. They told Dan they were reluctant to hold the two tables because Charlene had yet to pay the*

*$25,000 for the event several months ago and the $1,000 contribution for the year. She also had not signed the pledge commitment for the $30,000 capital campaign contribution. Dan was surprised. He told them to send a statement to Charlene regarding all of these, and they told him that they already had, several times. They had even called her twice to discuss the situation; she apologized the first time, and then recently shoved the situation aside by saying that she had some concerns.*

*Dan called Charlene.*

**Dan:** (After some small talk) *"I'm actually calling to follow up on your commitment for two tables for the benefit. Thank you so much for this generous gift! It will really help a lot. But, I've been informed by the staff that before we can reserve your two tables on our list as a commitment, you'll need to take care of your other outstanding obligations first. There's the $25,000 payment from your event several months ago and then your annual contribution of $1,000. We also need your signature on the $30,000 capital campaign pledge and to set a date for that payment."*

**Charlene:** *"Actually, Dan, I have some concerns about what's been happening regarding the outreach program. I've heard from several people in the community that they don't think it's truly open to everyone."*

*Dan and Charlene discussed this issue at great length and Dan resolved to look into it. They never got back to the discussion of Charlene's outstanding pledges.*

*Time continued to pass with no resolution and the benefit was getting closer and closer. Finally, Dan discussed the situation with the members of the executive committee and recommended that they give Charlene a last chance to make good on her financial commitments and if she had not done so by the next committee meeting, then they would take this as her resignation. The executive committee concurred.*

**Dan:** *"Charlene, you've been such an enthusiastic board member. But I've talked to the executive committee and you need to give this some really hard thought. You must resolve your financial commitments by the next committee meeting. If we don't receive these payments by then, we will accept your resignation. I do hope that it won't come to this."*

*A fax arrived moments before the executive committee in which Charlene stated that she was resigning from the board, effective immediately. Not wanting to let Charlene off the hook, a letter was sent to her from Dan on behalf of the organization accepting her resignation, stating:*

> *We hope that you will continue to be engaged with our organization at a level that is comfortable for you. Although we are not expecting to receive any of your previous financial commitments at this time, if circumstances change, we will welcome them. We hope to see you at our events in the future and we have valued your time dedicated to our organization.*

## What Could Have Been Done?

In this case, even if proper vetting and onboarding had taken place, it may not have reflected empty promises from past board service or prevented the behavior. However, this makes the case for ensuring that these activities are done consistently for everyone so it at least gives the board chair or responsible party the ability to say:

"You were aware of and committed to these financial obligations and failed to fulfill them." If the board member can't argue ignorance after the fact, there is no opportunity to blame someone else for his or her failure to deliver.

No one, not even Dan, dug deeper to find out more about Charlene's "other concerns" and whether or not they were valid or how to resolve them so her service and commitment could continue.

### Solution Strategy: Now What?

The actual intervention — confronting the behavior, giving the board member a chance to resolve it on her own by making the payments, and then taking final action if she didn't do so — was handled by the staff, the board chair, and the executive committee in a decisive and necessary manner, albeit uncomfortable.

Closing the loop, in addition to the board chair's letter, requires four more steps. First, a review of the recruitment and onboarding process is in order to see if anything else could have been done or should now be added. Second, the chair, on behalf of the board, should go back to Joe to address any bad feelings or concerns. Joe did suggest bringing this person on board and he may be feeling uncomfortable, angry, or guilty for how things turned out.

Third, the board chair, the governance committee chair, or Joe (as her friend), should reach out to Charlene to find out what her specific concerns were with the outreach program or additional aspects of the organization's work so they can avoid those concerns coming from others in the future. If anything, Charlene could serve as a reality check for the board in the event that these concerns were valid and not just an excuse to refrain from fulfilling the pledges that she made.

And fourth, after an appropriate amount of time, the board could perhaps find a way to re-engage Charlene on a more controlled or limited basis: inviting Charlene to be Dan's guest at an event; asking her opinion or input on a specific issue; seeing if she could volunteer on a special project; or anything else that could salvage and rebuild the relationship.


### BEHAVIOR: UNDERMINES THE BOARD CHAIR

**Definition:** Undermining means to weaken or sabotage someone through either subtle or obvious means. When a board member undermines the board chair he or she is challenging the board chair's authority to delegate and facilitate in leading the governance process.

**Impact:** This behavior can create poor interpersonal relationships on the board, encourage the development of factions or cliques, and even harm the constructive partnership between the board chair and the chief executive. More than anything, it might encourage the board chair to change his or her leadership style in a way that is not beneficial to the rest of the group or even cause the board chair to leave the board altogether.

**Case:** *Jill Jones and David Davidson were two very different people and their contributions to the board were unique, but equally strong. Jill was young, worked hard to cheerlead the* *board, and had great relationships with board members and the chief executive. Jill served as the development committee chair and one of her responsibilities was the annual benefit. David was older, more of a father figure. He offered valuable perspective and experience. He served as the finance committee chair and brought a needed expertise.*

*Jill admits that originally she and David started off on the wrong foot. She noticed that for some reason, David acted competitively towards her. And, he subtly put Jill down in front of the other board members.*

*The time came to develop the slate of nominees for officers for the next term. Board members were privately saying to Jill that they were going to nominate her for the board chair position because she showed great leadership and had a positive attitude. And because of her strong relationship with the chief executive, it seemed a natural fit.*

*Jill was voted the new chair. After she was elected, she found out that David had been saying privately to other board members that he didn't think she was the right person for the job. It became clear that David had actually wanted the job, and was put out that his name didn't come up naturally in the nomination process.*

*Once Jill became chair, David upped his attacks. He would disagree with just about everything in a meeting, especially if Jill was supporting a certain action or position. Eventually another board member took David aside and told him to stop. David was apologetic and backed down. But after that, he just became distant towards Jill in particular, and disengaged himself almost completely from the board. He would come to meetings, but his participation had waned.*

*Recently, Jill heard that David will be traveling extensively for the coming year. He had casually mentioned this months and months ago, but never told anyone that he was actually doing it or when. Everyone felt that David was pretty cavalier about just taking off like that, without discussing his absence with Jill or the chief executive or finding a way to cover for his absence. Jill had to appoint an interim finance chair to take over David's responsibilities and started to think about who they would get to replace him on the board. Then, through the grapevine, Jill heard that in David's view, he hadn't resigned from the board — he was just taking a break. David fully intends to be active on the board when he returns, whenever that might be.*

## What Could Have Been Done?

In the very beginning, when Jill acknowledged that she had gotten off to the wrong start with David, she may have had an opportunity to work at repairing the situation in a more proactive manner by speaking with him further about it offline, or even getting the then-board chair involved.

Having a clear succession policy would have helped to alleviate the sense of competition David had towards Jill when the time came for officer elections. In taking leadership cultivation and planning more seriously, with predeveloped criteria and timelines, the process may ultimately be more thorough and transparent, and feel fairer to everyone involved.

## Solution Strategy: Now What?

The good news is that the active undermining of Jill as chair and the competition for her role has relief for the time being. Jill will have a chance to focus on being chair and serving the organization appropriately without the tension of David's presence.

David has proven that he is unwilling to work under Jill's leadership, and that he has lost interest in staying committed. The most reasonable solution at this point would be for the governance committee to ask David to step down from the board for the time being, making sure that he has accepted and understood that he is a negative force. This will be a difficult conversation to have, and should be handled with grace and sensitivity. The board should have a clear policy regarding the removal of a board member for failure to honor his or her responsibilities and, ideally, David would have been informed of this policy when he began his term. David's departure should be followed up with a communiqué acknowledging his unacceptable absence and stating for the record that it constitutes a resignation. It can also be stressed that there is the sincere hope (if appropriate and desirable) that he will let the board know when he returns so they can mutually determine to what extent he could become re-engaged.

Jill may want to suggest some time for the board to do teamwork surrounding the loss of David as a team member. This is an often-overlooked process that can provide enormous closure to a team and open new doors for the future. When a team member leaves, especially after being asked to step down, there will be different feelings among the other members of the board. If these thoughts and concerns are acknowledged and openly discussed, the previous version of the team can be retired and the new team can start with a clean slate.

## BEHAVIOR: INSISTS ON PERSONAL OPINION IN THE FACE OF MAJORITY DECISIONS

**Definition:** When a board member fails to contribute to the team decision-making process by "fighting for" something that the group has already decided against.

**Impact:** When a board member refuses to bow to majority decision it causes high frustration among the group, wastes time and energy, and ultimately lowers the value of the individual's contributions because the other board members will consider him or her an obstacle to the team.

**Case:** *Evelyn Ewing is driving the board nuts. She came on about three years ago, is very bright, comes to every meeting, is always well prepared, and truly cares about the organization. But the rest of the board is definitely Evelyn-fatigued.*

*This board is a policy-making board and each member was appointed. Because of the nature of the organization, the board must review and make policy decisions on a frequent basis. Every time an issue comes up, Evelyn insists on discussing it to death. Our meetings take twice as long as they should. Then, when we do come to a decision, Evelyn will not rest even if she is the lone dissenter. She continues to fight the decision, both in the meeting and offline, and will bring it up again and again at future meetings. Her colleagues on the board are very polite and try to be respectful, but there comes a point where something just has to be done!*

### Solution Strategy: Now What?

An effective board moves to an understanding and articulation of its collective power; one board equals one voice. The board must work in such a way as to make decisions and exercise authority through the blending of individual viewpoints. Once a full discussion has happened, a vote has been taken, and a majority opinion has been made, it is imperative that all board members support that decision both publicly and privately. If a board member does not support a decision for whatever reason, she has a responsibility to remain silent or step down from the board.

In Evelyn's case, the board chair needs to have an intervention, and probably should have done so sooner. Just because someone is appointed (or even elected) to the board, does not mean she has the right to hold court. If the board chair has no success in broaching the subject with the board member privately, the chair could adopt a strategy in the public forum, such as the following:

**Evelyn:** *"Madam Chairman, I would like to bring up the issue of the policy we voted on last week. As you know, I am on the record as opposing this policy and really think we need to revisit it. For example, I've been thinking about..."*

**Board chair:** *"Excuse me, Evelyn. I want to thank you for your continued concern about this issue. We have explored this issue extensively and are now on record with a decision. The vote last month was 9–1 against. It will only be reopened for discussion upon the receipt in writing of significant factual data that warrants such."*

Handled in this direct manner, it will be made clear to Evelyn that unless she has additional support from other board members or strong evidence that a decision was made without the appropriate information at hand, matters once discussed and voted upon will be closed once and for all.

## BEHAVIOR: CRITICIZES THE ORGANIZATION IN PUBLIC

**Definition:** When a board member, who by nature of the position should be a public ambassador for the organization he or she serves, makes critical or disparaging comments about the board, the organization as a whole, or another affiliated person.

**Impact:** In addition to being indiscreet and possibly sharing confidential information, an organization's reputation and public good will can be compromised by this behavior.

**Case:** *Danielle Deakins was having dinner at one of the power restaurants in town. She was talking to her dinner companions about Be a Better Family, the organization whose board she had joined a year ago.*

**Danielle:** *"All I can say is that the organization is really not what I thought it would be — especially the chief executive. I just don't like her style. I find her very pushy and too bubbly all the time. And I really do not agree with the new program she has the staff working on. I don't see how it can possibly be successful and it's going to cost a lot of money that we just don't have. I really think she's going to run the organization out of business!"*

*Danielle did not realize that her conversation was being overheard by the next table. Unfortunately, it was the best friend of the chief executive, who also happened to be a reporter.*

### Solution Strategy: Now What?

Lucky for the organization as a whole, the reporter is a friend of the chief executive and most likely wouldn't put her in a negative spotlight. The board chair should be informed of the situation immediately and then have a serious conversation with the troublesome board member. Having the specific factual information — place, date, time, and who heard what — is the only way this conversation can have legitimacy. It cannot be hearsay. Speaking poorly of the organization in public, regardless of whether or not confidential information is publicized, is an unacceptable behavior and the board member should be confronted and held accountable.

### After-the-Fact Conversation Starter

**Board chair:** *"Danielle, something's come to my attention and it's a little embarrassing. You were overheard at The Place Restaurant on March 17 around 8 p.m. talking about Be a Better Family and Judy, our chief executive. Unfortunately, someone heard you say that you weren't comfortable with the organization or with Judy and that you had concerns about our program focus and financial stability.*

*"I bring this up for two reasons. The first is that we really have to be careful about what we say when we are in public and to whom. The person who overheard this happens to be a reporter. What you said really wasn't something substantial enough to be reported publicly, but it may raise other unfounded questions that our organization might have to deal with. The other reason is that if this gets back to Judy it can really cause some demoralization and may compromise your relationship with her. I would feel better if you could discuss your concerns with me, and maybe we can even take them to Judy in a diplomatic way."*

## SERVING DUAL INTERESTS

A conflict of interest occurs when a board member has a professional or personal interest that interferes with his or her independent decision making. These types of actual conflicts of interest prevent board members from fulfilling their duty of loyalty to the organization — placing the wellness of the organization above other considerations. Perceived conflicts of interest, if not addressed, generate an *appearance of impropriety* that can ultimately lower the public's confidence in the organization. It is up to the board to be sensitive to this perception and determine how to deal with it.

Conflicts of interest may spawn many different kinds of troublesome behaviors. It is extremely important to look to the root of the behaviors and, when a conflict of interest is involved, it must be addressed in an open and transparent manner. The following troublesome behaviors can become problematic conflicts of interest if not managed appropriately. Some or all of these measures could be taken to prevent the behaviors from forming:

- Maintain a clearly stated and comprehensive conflict-of-interest policy that is distributed, reviewed, and signed annually by each board member, along with a process for disclosure. All board members need to be properly educated to understand what conflicts of interest are, how to disclose potential conflicts appropriately, and the consequences for not doing so.

- Maintain a clearly stated and comprehensive code of ethics that is distributed, reviewed, and signed annually by each board member.

- It should be made absolutely clear to all board members from day one that they are there to serve the interests of the organization, not themselves or anyone else related to the cause. If it becomes apparent that someone is there for the wrong reasons, he or she must be given a choice to either leave the board or commit for the right reasons.

- Board members must recognize in advance that their service cannot and will not bring them direct financial return in any way.

- Be sure the bylaws cover contingencies for board member removal (such as the failure to maintain confidentiality).

- The governance committee should consider occasional leadership development activities around loyalty to mission and duty of care.

Some of the behaviors below suggest more specific preemptive solutions and all will require additional action. Keep the list on the previous page in mind as you read the specific cases and their solution strategies.

## BEHAVIOR: FAILS TO MAINTAIN CONFIDENTIALITY

**Definition:** When a member of the board fails to maintain the best interests of the organization by publicly sharing aspects of organizational business that legally and ethically require nondisclosure.

**Impact:** This troublesome behavior causes potential damage to the organization's image and public good will. Depending on the nature of the organization and its work, it could impact staff records, client/patient records, and may even bring legal actions or cause a loss of business opportunity.

**Case:** *Sean Scott was the head of human resources for a very large nonprofit. Handling benefits was a huge part of her job. Because of the numbers of employees, Sean regularly used brokers to find the best plans for the organization when policies were being renegotiated.*

*In the past, Sean found that using three different brokers usually got a competitive spread of bids for consideration by the board. This particular year one of the brokers, Gene, who usually provided bids, was now serving on the board. Gene thought he should still be able to solicit bids for the organization. Sean was concerned about a potential conflict of interest and discussed it with the chief executive, who also reviewed the conflict-of-interest policy. Technically, since Gene was only requesting to obtain bids and wasn't getting business out of it, he could be part of the bidding process. If one of his bidders got the contract, however, it was agreed that Gene would resign. Sean reported this back to Gene who said, "Absolutely — if one of my companies has the successful bid, I will most definitely step down from the board."*

*As part of the bidding process, brokers send out requests for bids from the insurance carriers they have worked with in the past. Gene really wanted the business, so he sent requests for bids to every single insurance carrier he could think of. The other two brokers couldn't get bids because Gene had flooded the market.*

*The two other brokers complained to Sean. Seeing the problem, Sean came up with a solution that she took to the chief executive. She reasoned that there were six top insurance companies that were likely to have the most competitive bids. What if they assigned two insurance companies to each of the three brokers? This would make it a fair process.*

*It was determined that the chief executive should handle this situation since Gene was not acting in his capacity as a board member, but rather in the capacity of a vendor to the organization. The chief executive called Gene and told him about the solution they had come up with and asked Gene for the two carriers he wanted to use. Gene gave them, but he wasn't happy about it. He felt that the chief executive had overstepped his boundaries (and frankly, did not respect the fact that, after all, he WAS a board member). So when the deadline arrived to submit the bids, Gene did not submit the bids from the two insurance carriers he was to represent. Sean was forced to go ahead with the process and they made their selection from among the four bids received.*

*While all of this was going on, the organization was also involved in another major initiative. It had decided to spin off part of the organization's programs into a social entrepreneurship venture that would be designed to bring in a revenue stream to the nonprofit. The board had concluded that the chief executive was the only person uniquely qualified to lead the new venture. It was voted that he would do so as soon as a national search could be conducted to find his replacement as the new chief executive for the nonprofit.*

*There was a competitive aspect to the new venture, so the board and the senior staff had been reminded of the need for strict confidentiality under stated organizational policies. However, Gene was so angry about the chief executive "causing him a loss of business" that he gave a television interview laying out the plans regarding this venture and implied that the chief executive orchestrated this initiative for personal gain.*

## What Could Have Been Done?

Gene could have been given a choice from the very beginning: Keep his position on the board and refrain from acting as a broker, or resign from the board so that he could participate as a broker in the bid process.

There was no need for the board to have been involved in the insurance bid process, as it was a management issue. However, since a board member was involved, the board chair should have been made aware of the issue from the start.

## Solution Strategy: Now What?

Gene violated the board confidentiality policy by going public regarding the new venture and making derogatory remarks about the organization; therefore, his termination from the board should be effective immediately.

Because the board had also done due diligence in supporting the decision to move forward with the new venture and employ the chief executive to head the project, there was no need to cover old ground and give any credence to Gene's claim of personal gain by the chief executive.

While there may have been intervention points throughout the case in which the behavior could have been dealt with, prevention was really the way to ensure that this case did not play out as it did. When someone feels wronged, the fight or flight impulse kicks in. But, Gene intentionally did harm to the organization.

Situations like this also suggest that organizations consider media training for both board and staff, as well as the development of a crisis plan to deal with any kind of emergency that may affect the organization's ability to operate. While this case dealt with a public relations and good will challenge, conducting scenario planning for a wide variety of contingencies will limit future stress and allow the board to better handle any situation if and when a crisis erupts.

## FOOD FOR THOUGHT

*"Too often, charter school board members mistakenly believe that the authority which the board possesses to govern the school is possessed by each board member individually. It is not. Some board members go so far as to behave as if what they want accomplished individually is the same as what the board wants accomplished. A friend who is an authorizer told me of a comical example of this: A board member ordered the school leader to install a bicycle rack because she wanted her child to ride a bike to school!"*

Brian L. Carpenter, Executive Director, National Charter Schools Institute, Mt. Pleasant, MI

## BEHAVIOR: SERVES PERSONAL INTERESTS OR MULTIPLE LOYALTIES

**Definition:** When someone commits to board service, he or she is agreeing to the principle that the good of the organization will govern all decision making. A board member's role is to put aside any personal preferences. Something is troublesome when an individual board member fails to recognize or fulfill this duty and attempts to serve his or her own personal interests first.

**Impact:** The board member undermines himself or herself as an impartial voice on the board. Decision making is flawed. Public trust is at risk or damaged.

**Case:** *Ginny Glass was elected to her community's school board. Ginny understood when she was elected that her role on the board was to help set and ensure adherence to policy. She also wanted to serve because she felt that she would have the ability to have a say in the school's management while her children were still students.*

*The athletic policy for the school was quite specific:*

- *Our athletic department will strive to develop and maintain a comprehensive athletic program using coaches who strive to treat student athletes fairly.*

- *The athletic program will seek the highest development of each student athlete.*

- *The athletic program will be committed to high standards of ethics, sportsmanship, and personal conduct, and will respect the individual dignity of every athlete.*

- *The athletic program will be conducted in such a way as to reinforce it as an educational activity.*

*Toward that end, and specifically with regard to field hockey, it was stated that all eligible student athletes below the varsity level shall get equal playing time. At the varsity level, playing time will be as fair as possible while still allowing the team to be competitive.*

*Ginny's daughter, Emily, is on the field hockey team but isn't one of the best. This year, because she is a junior, Emily has moved up to varsity level. Emily came home sobbing one evening saying that Coach Chuck made an embarrassing comment about her performance in front of the whole team. She told her mom that she was convinced she wouldn't be starting at the first game of the season.*

*Ginny knew it was unlikely that Emily would start, but felt that the coach had violated the athletic policy all the same. She felt that Coach Chuck had exhibited poor personal conduct and that he had failed to treat Emily with the respect and dignity she deserved. Ginny immediately called the parents of the other team members, asking them to come to her house for a meeting that night to discuss something of vital importance to the school. She presented her concerns. Some of the parents were indignant and encouraged Ginny to take up the issue at the upcoming school board meeting. Others in the room were surprised to hear something like this. Coach Chuck had been the varsity field hockey coach for the past five years and in three of those years, the team had won the league championship. They had never heard this kind of complaint against Coach Chuck before and wanted specifics.*

*Ginny said that she couldn't repeat the comments — they were too horrible to say in polite company. She also then implied that Coach Chuck probably shouldn't be coaching the girls team "…if you know what I mean."*

*Over the course of the next few weeks, the stories ran wild in the school and the community and two distinct camps developed — one in favor of Coach Chuck and one against him. To make matters worse, not only was Emily not one of the starters at the opening varsity game, but she never got a chance to play at all.*

*The next week, Ginny insisted that the board have a special closed session to discuss whether or not Coach Chuck should remain as the coach of the team. After the meeting, there was a public vote and Coach Chuck was immediately removed. Later, one of the parents heard Coach Chuck say, "I still don't know what they think it is I did wrong. No one, not even the superintendent, asked me what all this was about. When I had asked to see him to talk about it, he said that it had already been elevated to the board level and that there were serious charges that needed to be addressed."*

## What Could Have Been Done?

One former board chair of a private elementary school said that at his first meeting as chair, he started with: *"If there is anyone here who came on this board because you thought it would give you an extra advantage with regard to your child at this school, I am here to say that it not only will not, it should not. You have accepted an obligation as a trustee to put the school's interests first even if it may be in conflict with what you perceive to be in your child's personal best interest. If you can't accept that, then you have to give this some hard thought."* He said that one woman looked at him with tears in her eyes, saying, *"But I thought that being on the board would put me in a position to directly help my daughter. I don't know if I want to be on the board if I can't use my role to do so."* The board chair replied, *"Well, then you have a decision to make."* She ultimately resigned.

Ginny should have gone straight to the chair of the school board and the superintendent to discuss her concern, not to fellow parents. Involving the athletic director and Coach Chuck himself could have prevented an uproar in the community and the loss of a quality coach.

The actions and inactions of the chief executive (i.e., the superintendent) in this case were also at fault. The superintendent is the paid professional who offers insight and guidance to the volunteer board regarding situations between teachers and coaches on the one side and students and parents on the other. The superintendent failed to pull the right people together to ferret out the escalated problem.

**Solution Strategy: Now What?**

The concept of an elected (or appointed) school board is based on the notion that schools belong to local communities. While they hire professionals to administer and to teach, ultimately, the local community has a say in the governance of that school.

This is a good sentiment, but sometimes the fact that these are "elected" board members may actually contribute to poor governance. The risk involved is that parents run for election (or seek appointment) because of the vested interest in their children as students, and it means that unqualified people are sometimes put into these positions of authority and influence. While an elected (or even an appointed) school board is technically representing a nonprofit, there is a unique character to it that begs its own considerations. Unfortunately, when dealing with parents of children, one of the hardest things for them to understand is that once they assume the role of board member they must take off their parent hat and put on their "in the best interests of the school" hat in order for the board to be effective.

While Ginny acted as many concerned parents might, she abused her role as a school board member by calling a private meeting of parents. They may have attended the meeting thinking she was acting in some official capacity rather than as a concerned parent. Airing her concerns to them first, without following an established protocol, contributed to making the situation far worse.

Again, prevention is the key to the solution in this case. Proper orientation for incoming board members regarding roles and responsibilities and working within established procedures may have prevented Ginny from acting in the way that she did. But after the fact, this board should review those procedures to ensure that they are both proactively preventative and logically reactive to address situations of this kind. Increasing their individual and collective understanding of how a board must serve a mission would be helpful. Finally, training around the constructive partnership between the board and the superintendent (any chief executive) is suggested.

---

## FOOD FOR THOUGHT

*"It's critical that each board member be focused on the best way to achieve the goals of the organization and not on his or her own agenda. This should be taken into consideration when selecting new board members. During the recruitment process, some of the questions should be designed to specifically address this issue such as 'What is your specific interest in serving on this board?' or 'Have you ever served on another board where a board member used his or her position for professional or personal gain? If so, can you tell us about that and what happened?' Listening carefully to what and how a potential board candidate answers can assist in finding the most qualified persons to fill the seats."*

Rebecca J. Rush, Financial Advisor, Houston, Texas

## BEHAVIOR: SEEKS OR RECEIVES INAPPROPRIATE FINANCIAL RETURN FROM AFFILIATION

**Definition:** When a board member engages in a financial transaction with the organization and receives remuneration that is disproportionate to the services provided, or uses his or her affiliation with the organization to gain financial benefits in any other way (he or she is accepting private benefit or inappropriate private inurement). Technically, if policies are aptly followed and disclosure is appropriately made, board members can engage in financial transactions in an organization. However, the ethical perception should be seriously considered.

**Impact:** If handled inappropriately, the board member, as well as any other board member involved in the decision, could be penalized with excise taxes.

**Case:** *Vin Vernon was nominated to be on the board of directors of a very old and very large prestigious national organization. When the governance committee reviewed Vin's nomination, it thought he looked pretty good on paper. At the interview, it seemed like he was exactly the kind of person they wanted affiliated with the organization. He was prominent in his community and represented an untapped geographic area.*

*Early into Vin's board service reports came back that he was using the name of the organization in such a way as to secure personal business, and in one case that a bank had actually given Vin a loan based on his affiliation with the board! The board chair and the chief executive discussed this situation and asked the governance committee to reinterview Vin and ask him directly about what had been heard.*

*At the meeting, Vin vehemently denied it. The governance committee was relieved, but took the opportunity to remind him of all of his obligations as a board member (including making a personal contribution and raising funds, neither of which Vin had yet done). They reminded him about the organization's conflict-of-interest policy and code of ethics, stating, for the record, that if any real evidence of anything like this was discovered with any board member, the committee would have to recommend a vote for removal.*

*As time went on, Vin had not done any fundraising nor had he made a personal financial contribution. The reports continued that Vin was still doing the same thing in using his affiliation with the organization for personal gain. And then the organization was provided with undeniable proof. The governance committee met immediately and recommended removal. Vin, as was provided for in the board's bylaws and policies, requested an appeal to the full board. This was provided, and the case was heard before the full board with Vin given an opportunity to address the board. Ultimately, the board voted removal.*

### Solution Strategy: Now What?

This board had policies, a structure, and a process in place that allowed necessary action to take place in order to preserve the organization's good name. Vin was given first the benefit of the doubt and a clear warning of the expectations for future behavior. When evidence was presented that he was violating policy, the board proceeded with what needed to be done, which was removal.

What we don't know is *"…the rest of the story."* An additional cautionary tale here would be for the board to have a crisis plan to deal with any possible negative publicity that may have resulted from Vin's removal. Sometimes individuals will pursue revenge tactics even when they are in the wrong. At best it could be dealing with unflattering or nasty comments made to a journalist. At worst, it could lead to violence. Prior to removal of a board member, organizations should develop a contingency plan just in case there are unfortunate consequences resulting from the action.

# Chapter 3: Poor People Skills and Personality Conflicts

An *adage* is a proverb or wise saying made familiar by long use. Consider the following:

- Beauty is only skin deep.

- You can't teach an old dog new tricks.

- All that glitters is not gold.

- Where there's smoke there's fire.

- We boil at different degrees.

- You can lead a horse to water but you can't make it drink.

These adages, among others, demonstrate the challenges of poor people skills and personality conflicts. The behaviors addressed in this chapter have less to do with a failure to fulfill board member responsibilities. These troublesome scenarios are tied more closely to personal characteristics or clashing personalities that make it difficult to form solid relationships and work well in a team atmosphere. As a result, board teamwork is damaged, group decisions are compromised, and board discussions are hindered. Because these behaviors stem from personality development, idiosyncrasies, poor training or skill development, or personal responses to actual or perceived conflict, they are unfortunately more difficult to prevent or change.

## DAMAGED BOARD WORK

Similar to the "uncollective" board process in Chapter 2, damaged board teamwork is the result of the following behaviors. When board members are motivated by their own individual opinions rather than working to form a group stance on a particular issue or decision, it shows disrespect for the group's diversity of knowledge, opinion, and motivation, and prevents teamwork from happening efficiently or at all. Some or all of the following measures could be taken to prevent the behaviors from forming:

- All potential board members should be fully vetted in the recruitment process, particularly when they are recommended over and over again from the same source. To vet properly:

  - Ask questions to get a sense of whether or not an individual works well in a group.

  - Look for individuals who can keep an open mind and see different sides to an issue.

  - Keep an eye out for signs of a strong ego (has he or she been able to serve in a nonleadership role on another board successfully?) and make a few discreet inquiries if need be.

- A discussion on team theory and how decisions are reached and honored should take place during the orientation and onboarding process. All board members should know the consequences of failing to work together as a team.

- Meeting etiquette should be discussed during recruitment and orientation, as well as the consequences of not adhering to it.

- Maintain an overall board understanding of the expectations and limitations of board-staff relationships.

- Create job descriptions for the board as a whole, individual board members, board officers, and committees so there is no misunderstanding regarding specific roles and responsibilities.

- Time should be spent annually on team-building and leadership development exercises to ensure an understanding and commitment to group work.

Some of the behaviors below suggest more specific preemptive solutions and all will require additional action. Keep the above in mind as you read the specific cases and their solution strategies.

## BEHAVIOR: DOESN'T WORK AS A TEAM PLAYER

**Definition:** When a board member determines that he or she knows best and declines or refuses to participate in group discussions or decision making. Often, he or she will complete tasks without input from the rest of the board.

**Impact:** This behavior is irritating and demotivating, and can cost the organization time and money by making decisions that are not authorized and/or by duplicating efforts. When a board member refuses to gather team insight, his or her board work will lack a diversity of knowledge and opinion and could lose sight of the important issues. The board member might also end up wasting his or her own time if the rest of the board decides to redo the work as a team.

**Case:** *Neil Nathan, Katie Knight, Wendy Warren, and Travis Trent were part of the governance committee. One of their responsibilities as a committee was to come up with a roster of leadership development activities for the next year over the course of five upcoming meetings. The board as a whole wanted to work on the specific issues implied in The Sarbanes-Oxley Act and asked the committee to prepare a report for the next meeting with a schedule and speaker or study group recommendation on how these issues could be tackled. Travis was the committee chair. He told Neil, Katie, and Wendy that he would contact them to set up a conference call within the next week to discuss next steps. One week stretched to two, and when Travis finally called, the only time all of them could meet was one week before the upcoming board meeting, which was cutting it close.*

*When they finally did talk, Travis started out by saying, "Good news — I've completed the roster and I've even got the speakers all lined up." He told them that there really wasn't any point to having a lengthy call and promised to e-mail them the roster before the board meeting. He did, the day of the meeting. When it came time to present the information, Travis did so without including the others. Unfortunately, it didn't appear that Travis really understood The Sarbanes-Oxley Act. One of the topics and speakers was on fundraising and he did not include a segment on document retention and destruction!*

## What Could Have Been Done?

Did committee members receive any training on committee responsibility? Were any staff members considered to support the committee efforts?

Did the other committee members speak up when they hadn't heard anything from Travis? All board members, committee members or not, should be holding each other accountable for their work.

## Solution Strategy: Now What?

The board chair should be informed of the situation and then should talk to Travis about the value of utilizing committees and involving others in committee work; after all, isn't that the point of having a committee in the first place? Why set up a working group if not everyone assigned to it will be involved? Travis could have benefited from the input of the others to ensure that the roster was complete and on topic.

Good board practices suggest that a formal process should be put in place for electing committee chairs and for conducting regular evaluations regarding the need for committees and the work of the committee members.

### BEHAVIOR: HAS SIDEBARS WITH OTHERS IN MEETINGS OR OFFLINE CONVERSATIONS

**Definition:** In this context, a sidebar is a private conversation held during a group meeting but among a smaller portion of the group. Offline conversations are those among a smaller group of people outside of the boardroom that predebate or continue to debate issues that were discussed openly in a group meeting. Often, sidebars and offline conversations are lobbying attempts to undermine others, redirect or refocus group energies, change decisions already made, or develop or solidify factions or cliques within a group.

**Impact:** In a meeting, a sidebar conversation harms the focus of the entire group, as well as those who are speaking privately, and prevents the group from thinking and deliberating together. Meeting etiquette requires that each board member listens to the others, and when someone has something to offer or share, to do so with the full group so that everyone is working from the same information. When a smaller group has a private discussion in a public meeting, those involved come to incomplete or flawed opinions or conclusions regarding the topic because they have missed the other voices in the room. Additionally, offline conversations do not benefit from the entire group's input and so others may form opinions or frame decisions that are not under team consensus. Both forms of conversation undermine the board as a whole, and may cause unrest between board members.

**Case:** *Paul Porter and Pat Peters always sat together at meetings. They frequently discussed the agenda topics in whispered conversation while others were discussing the same topics in the open forum. They also spent time outside of the boardroom discussing various aspects of what happened at the last meeting or what would be addressed at the* *next meeting. In one instance, Paul felt strongly that the organization was going in the wrong direction on the upcoming capital campaign. Of the three firms that had presented at the last meeting, Paul thought they should go with The Arrow Group rather than The Funding Connection. He was convinced, based on what the other board members were saying at the last meeting, that The Funding Connection was going to be voted in. After discussing it with Pat, they decided that the board needed to review this further and they prepared a presentation for the next meeting on why The Arrow Group should be engaged. When they got to the meeting they were surprised to find that the minutes of the last meeting showed a recommendation that The Arrow Group be voted on in this meeting! They both wondered: How had they missed that?*

### Solution Strategy: Now What?

The board chair has a responsibility to stop sidebars from happening in meetings. He or she can speak to the board member(s) in question during a break or outside of the meeting and respectfully ask them to desist. Or, the board chair can address the behavior as it is happening within the meeting. The offending parties may not be aware of the distracting nature of their behavior and calling it to their attention shows common courtesy to the others in the meeting. Additionally, there should be an understanding among all board members that reflecting on board issues outside the boardroom can be a hindrance to the team. Board members should refrain from heated discussions offline when/if their opinions cannot be shared with the full board.

### After-the-Fact Conversation Starter

**Board chair:** (said outside of a meeting with each of the participants separately) *Paul, can I have a moment of your time? I've noticed that you and Pat are often having side conversations while we are in the middle of our meetings. You may not realize how distracting it can be and how difficult it is to hear what someone else is saying when you two are talking. And, we really need you both to focus on what others are saying so that we can get your reactions and input. I fear that you may be missing some of the meeting content and I know how much you are committed to what we do. We really need your full participation!*

**Board chair:** (in a meeting) *Paul, Pat — may I ask you to hold your thoughts to share with the entire group once Sam is finished speaking? We really need to hear from you both, but let's let everyone hear from Sam first and then we'll ask you to add your thoughts so we can all benefit from both pieces of the discussion.*

## BEHAVIOR: BULLIES OR DISPLAYS A CONTROLLING PERSONALITY

**Definition:** When a board member, especially one who is not in a position of authority, has an obsessive and inappropriate need or desire to control other people or situations and acts in a domineering, intimidating, or threatening manner in order to get his or her way.

**Impact:** This behavior causes ill will and compromised relationships on the board and possibly even with the staff, leading to a breakdown of trust and an inability to work together. It stifles the opinions and input of others, alienating fellow board members from what should be a group process. The others are discouraged by a feeling of working for someone rather than the important cause that brought them there in the first place. A board member with a controlling personality causes the board to miss out on the knowledge and insight of other board members, making passive stewards out of once-engaged board members.

**Case:** *Dale Denton came on the board at the suggestion of the chief executive. Dale had a background in the area of research that the organization served and everyone felt that this would give him great insight into the organization's products and services and strategic framework.*

*During his first two years of service, he was relatively quiet. He came to meetings and made significant financial contributions and when he did speak up, what he had to say was very helpful. When the organization moved forward with a major new initiative, Dale became more and more active and more vocal.*

*Bryce Boynton was the staff person in charge of the organization's research department. Dale worked on the board committee that provided editorial support to that department. It was an important committee because the organization had to represent to its members and subscribers that their information was timely and correct.*

*Each year, Bryce would prepare the annual work plan and process to solicit article contributors and research project reports for the annual publication. Last year, Dale was concerned that Bryce's methodology didn't reach out to enough potential contributors. He had sent Bryce a number of e-mails with additional suggestions on whom to call and where to advertise and even how to do a public service announcement.*

*It was time to issue the requests for proposals again for the coming year. Dale decided to talk to Phyllis Potter, the chief executive, to let her know that he didn't think Bryce was reaching out enough or to the right individuals. Phyllis talked to Bryce and he explained why he was doing it this way. It was actually an issue of available resources (staff hours and funding) and competing work priorities more than any disagreement with Dale's suggestions. Phyllis reported back to Dale, saying she felt that while it may not be the ideal way to do it, she was confident that Bryce was getting the job done in the best way possible considering stretched resources.*

*Dale wrote a scathing e-mail to Phyllis and Bryce and copied it to the entire board. He detailed the numerous ideas that he had offered and even went so far as to say that if it were a problem of hands to work and money to fund, he would volunteer the hours and even subsidize some of the advertising. He concluded with comments that were just shy of calling both Phyllis and Bryce inept and incompetent.*

*Jake Jenson, the board's chair, had no sooner opened the e-mail than he was on the phone to Dale. He told Dale that his e-mail and the tone in which he presented his information were extremely disconcerting. He pointed out that the e-mail, copied to the entire board, can have a long-term and very damaging effect on the board's relationship with the staff. Jake said he knew that Dale did not intend for the e-mail to be perceived in this way. But it will be. And the content of it — that he offered to make the organization stronger — only got lost because of the way it was addressed.*

*Dale was silent.*

**Jake:** *"I know this may be hard for you to hear, but do me a favor and give this some thought. I'll call you back in an hour."*

*An hour later, Jake called Dale back. Dale had taken time to think about what Jake said, and saw his point. He recognized that his zeal was intended to help, but his action was hurtful, and he said he would write another e-mail and apologize.*

*Dale did send an apology, as promised. But there were lingering effects of what he had done. Trust had been broken, and it took time to rebuild.*

### What Could Have Been Done?

Regardless of whether or not Dale was doing the right thing by getting so involved in the hands-on work and communicating directly with Bryce, he should have respected the chief executive's response to his initial concern. Sometimes board members simply don't have all the information about the real life, day-to-day juggling going on inside the organization as the paid staff struggles to get everything done with limited time and resources. In order to keep a strong and constructive partnership with the chief executive, members of the board need to trust and respect the executive's judgment in managing the organization.

### Solution Strategy: Now What?

Again, the staff members need to be the ones to fit all the pieces together because they are the ones who *have* all the pieces. The board chair handled this extremely well. He addressed the behavior, not the person or the issue (i.e., the content of the e-mail). He did it in a direct way and he gave Dale a chance to think. He also did not back down from following up and, had Dale not offered a solution to fix the problem, the board chair would have been the one to force the next step.

If the board chair had not immediately intervened, the damage to trust and relationships within the organization may not have been repaired quite as easily, if ever. When boards ignore or procrastinate in dealing with behaviors like this because of fear or apathy, they actually enable such behavior and allow it to worsen.

## SHODDY DECISION MAKING

The following behaviors stem from an unwillingness to keep an open mind. Whether through intentional or unintentional dishonesty, deceit, or inappropriate initiative, these situations compromise the decision-making ability of the entire group. Some or all of the following measures could be taken to prevent the behaviors from forming:

- Background checks and appropriate vetting by the governance committee should always be done during the recruitment stage.

- During recruitment and orientation, a discussion of the organization's current position on its lifecycle should clarify the history, present state in the appropriate context, and future goals for all new board members.

- Board evaluations — of all board members and board officers specifically — should be conducted regularly so that weak board leadership can be further developed or removed from the board when necessary.

Some of the behaviors on the following pages suggest more specific preemptive solutions and all will require additional action. Keep the above in mind as you read the specific cases and their solution strategies.

*"The St. Jude system uses a membership screening committee. It reviews all nominees for appropriate eligibility. If approved by [the committee], they are recommended to the board for appointment for an initial one-year term. At the end of the first year they meet again in front of the membership screening committee and are asked to report on their contributions (personal financial commitment, raising funds from others, raising friends) to St. Jude for that year. If acceptable, then they are appointed for a two-year term. The review process takes place again at the end of the two years. Then, if acceptable, they are appointed for a three-year term. At the end of every three-year term, every board member is reviewed. If they are still contributing, they are recommended for renewal for another three-year term. There are no term limits. Contributing board members are invited to stay on indefinitely once they are in the three-year cycle and each three-year review shows contribution. They can, of course, retire off the board at the end of any of those terms if they wish, but when we find someone good, we want them to stay involved."*

Richard C. Shadyac, Sr., Ex-Officio Board Member, ALSAC/St. Jude Children's Hospital, Memphis, TN

## BEHAVIOR: WON'T ACCEPT CHANGE

**Definition:** When a board member is closed-minded to something new or different and stands in the way of necessary growth and change.

**Impact:** As an organization grows and adapts to external changes, the work and structure of the board also needs to change in order to keep the organization successful and relevant in its community. When a board member gets in the way of necessary change, opportunities are lost and the organization could be at risk for stagnation.

**Case:** *Ronnie Redgrove and Connie Cook were friends who came on the board around the same time. The board chair, Tammy, and the chief executive, Vicki, knew them both. The performing arts organization had unique governance and operational considerations: An artistic organization by nature assumes some risk each year when planning a season. There are no guarantees that each artistic event or activity will be "publicly" successful, earning the projected revenue from ticket sales. Some events and activities don't generate any earned revenue at all. Defining "success" for an artistic organization is often highly subjective and takes like-minded people on a team who support a specifically understood and generally accepted articulation of its mission.*

*Historically, the organization did well both generating earned income and fundraising for contributed income. Over the past five years it generated surpluses and now the operating reserve, which had been originally planned as a "rainy day" fund, was substantial. Vicki felt that the time had come for the organization to stretch its wings a bit and take an artistic risk.*

*They had never commissioned an artistic work before. Vicki wanted to hire a promising young artist, Rob Roberts, to lead a group of other artists in a collaborative project to produce a mixed-arts event that would be unlike anything the organization had ever done*

— so new and different that it would be artistically compelling and surely create a buzz in the community.

Vicki and Rob worked on a budget and felt that, to do it right, the project would cost $100,000. The operating reserve currently had a balance of $243,000. Vicki felt that the $100,000 was an acceptable risk to present to the board. Vicki then went over the project and explained the associated costs to Tammy. They agreed to put it on the agenda at the next meeting.

Vicki made the presentation to the board with supporting documentation and a PowerPoint presentation showing some of Rob's previous work. She felt that she provided the board members with the information they needed to make a sound decision, and she was fairly confident they would say yes.

Ronnie listened to Vicki's presentation and felt a very sick feeling in her stomach. They had worked so hard to get the $243,000 in the bank. What would happen if they lost the entire amount and the project was a huge public relations flop? And if the board said yes this time, where would it lead next?

Connie, on the other hand, listened to Vicki's presentation with mounting excitement. To be part of something so creative and innovative would really put the organization at the top of the list of the cultural organizations in the community. Connie had been somewhat frustrated until now because it seemed like the organization was always playing it safe.

The debate was on. Both Ronnie and Connie were very vocal and highly persuasive about their individual views. The board was divided regarding the issue. Vicki became increasingly upset. Tammy didn't know what to do — things erupted so suddenly and unexpectedly. This was normally a very pleasant and polite board.

The topic was tabled. There was much discussion in the next two meetings and offline lobbying in between. No decision was made.

Rob waited and waited and eventually decided that maybe he should think about a project somewhere else. Connie became disgusted and resigned from the board. Ronnie was relieved and felt that it had all worked out for the best — they still had the entire reserve right where it should be. Tammy wondered what she may have done wrong. The board had gotten completely out of control over this. And Vicki felt she had learned a lesson — don't rock the boat and don't touch the reserve!

## What Could Have Been Done?

This is a case where the board would have benefited from bringing in a trained consultant/facilitator to walk the group through the new opportunity, starting with an evaluation and discussion about individual risk tolerance versus organizational risk tolerance. It is understandable that individual board members bring their own rooted values to a group decision-making process, but each person has an obligation to put those values aside. Every board member is there to listen with an open mind to new possibilities and work with the team to weigh pros and cons according to what makes the most sense for the organization at a particular time. When something so fundamentally new or different is being presented, a trained outsider can help to ensure a successful dialogue, provide an objective point of view, and lead the team to a group consensus.

The board chair and chief executive could also have done a better job in preparing the board for the concept, or even seeking their counsel prior to making the presentation. If they had first brought Rob into a meeting and allowed him to talk and demonstrate his work, it would have introduced the idea without forcing the decision-making process right after. The board chair and chief executive could have asked the full board whether or not it made sense to take the project to the next step with Rob, and then develop a business plan. This may have avoided some of the negative gut reactions from the more conservative faction of the board, as they would have had a chance to first consider the idea from an artistic (mission-fulfillment) viewpoint rather than a financial perspective.

Additionally, with unique organizations like this one, it is important to address special considerations in the board recruitment process. Had she been briefed in advance on the need for artistic organizations to take risks, Ronnie may have reacted differently. And, if board members were fully educated on the purpose of reserves and given examples of how the money could or should be used, the board chair may have received better buy-in from the group.

## Solution Strategy: Now What?

The board chair may wish to have a one-on-one conversation with Ronnie regarding the potential for new opportunities opening up in the future.

In order to work with the team to manage organizational change and individual board members' responses to it, it may also be useful for the chief executive and board chair to initiate an organizational assessment. Although a big undertaking, this process could help the board focus on which developmental stage or stages the organization is passing through and whether its current capacities are sufficient to sustain it at that stage. With data and feedback gathered from stakeholders and others externally connected to the organization and its community, rather than a big idea coming from a single person inside the organization, board members can collectively determine the need for change.

As part of ongoing leadership development, the board could gain additional insights into understanding organizational risk tolerance and planning for acceptable risk and situational deficits for a particular programmatic need. Inviting financial planners to meetings to explain concepts and mechanisms or representatives from other organizations that have successfully reorganized or expanded would be one way to accomplish this.

Additionally, in response to this specific case, the board chair should lead a special session or make time in the next meeting for a briefing of the board on the issue of reserves. Financial reserves act as a safeguard for rainy days and allow organizations to adjust to recurrent variances in income and expenses. Reserves allow an organization to continue activity in the face of unpredictable market forces, economic downshifts, natural disasters, or other unexpected expenses that aren't within the control of nonprofit managers. And, as in this case, financial reserves make it possible for an organization to seize an unprecedented opportunity such as financing a new venture, making an advantageous capital purchase, or expanding a program at an opportune time.

## Behavior: Creates Cliques and Group Divisions

**Definition:** When an individual board member's behavior causes the development of subgroups within the larger group, usually around an opinion, action step, or specific decision. Cliques work against another individual or individuals, whether it is intentional or not, to remove power from the other person(s).

**Impact:** This behavior creates unrest between board members and wears down the board chair. It disrupts the decision-making processes, causing lack of consensus and a tendency for each subgroup or faction to "fight" for its idea for the sake of winning, rather than listen with an open mind for the good of the cause. Ultimately, when board members expect board time to be consumed by incessant disagreement, engagement and commitment begin to wane.

**Case:** *Viola Vaughn was a young activist who passionately worked on a wide variety of issues. She was extremely flattered and excited when she was nominated to serve on the national board of an advocacy group that worked to strengthen one of the causes she deeply cared about.*

*It was the only organization of its kind and had a very large board comprised of respected elders, successful business representatives, and individuals who had served in public office. There was also a small contingent of others like her — young, passionate activists who wanted to make a difference.*

*In the beginning, the young activist board members often went out after the board meetings to discuss what had happened and talk strategy about possible future advocacy events. Viola hadn't gotten to know them all that well yet, but they always included her. After awhile, she noticed that John and Todd often criticized the board chair, Don, and seemed to be rallying the troops of the other young board members; and, as time went on, some of the older ones too. As far as Viola could see, Don worked very hard to balance all sides and occasional conservatism was a respectful honoring of the group process.*

*At the next meeting, it was clear that dissention was brewing. John made a motion, which Todd seconded, for the organization to take a specific stand on a very controversial issue. It was clear that not everyone had a deep understanding or decided view of this issue. This bold move to get the organization to sanction this position was a radical departure of the organization's traditionally middle-of-the-road approach.*

*Viola felt that this issue was being used as subtext for something else. It was clear that there was a growing faction within the board regarding the manner in which the organization was being led. Viola saw that John and Todd were forming a contingent that was going to challenge Don's leadership. Until now, it appeared to be common knowledge among the board that Viola was a part of this group. She was uncomfortable with this realization so she went to Don and asked if she could talk about it.*

**Don:** *"Well, Viola. These guys are teaming up to make a good old power grab. It's unfortunate because it means that we are going to spend a lot of our upcoming time dealing with this as the central issue of our board meetings rather than doing the work we really should be doing."*

**Viola:** *"But can't we do something to stop it?"*

**Don:** *"Maybe I've just been around the block too many times, Viola, but I don't have the energy to mount a counterattack and I just don't want to play the game. If the rest of the organization wants to go in this direction, then I need to just bow out. I'll continue to work for the cause in another way."*

## Solution Strategy: Now What?

It is difficult to prevent a clique from forming — the nature of board work is to strategize, discuss difficult issues, and debate. It is the board chair's role to guide the discussion in the boardroom and talk to individuals separately if he or she sees the potential for cliques forming.

Unfortunately, there are some human behaviors or group dynamics that, once started, are difficult to reverse or control. In this case, unless there are others on the board who, like Viola, recognize what is happening and come together in a timely enough manner to bolster Don's leadership and offer alternative solutions, the clique will succeed. Sometimes cliques form and succeed for the right reasons, whether it is someone taking the lead to energize others to reengage a lethargic board, or in an attempt to change a founder-backed or rubber-stamping board. Other times, a clique's only success is leaving the board with a sour taste and lingering fallout.

Board members should be conscious of the possibility that fellow board members may attempt to create a faction against a specific activity, idea, or individual. One of a board member's individual responsibilities is to remain independent-minded within the group process and then, once a decision is made cohesively, to accept and support it on behalf of the entire board.

### BEHAVIOR: ACTS WITHOUT AUTHORITY

**Definition:** When a board member determines for himself or herself that he or she knows best and either participates in group discussions in a domineering manner, or acts without delegation or authorization outside of the board context to make something happen.

**Impact:** This behavior can be irritating and demotivating and in many cases can cost the organization time and money by taking programs or decisions in the wrong direction.

**Case:** *Mark Mann just joined the Local History Museum board. He has been a docent at the museum for over 10 years. He was delighted when the director of volunteers recommended him to the governance committee as a possible candidate for the board. He was anxious to help and decided that it would be great if the organization had a program that offered genealogy research for local residents. He decided to call it the "Create a Family Tree Campaign" and went online to find out how the museum could offer this to area residents. Mark found that basic kits could be ordered wholesale, so he ordered 100 for the museum. He paid with his own credit card, but assumed that he could get reimbursed. He then decided that the best day to do this would be the Saturday of Memorial Day weekend, just six weeks away. He called the local newspaper and asked it to run a story about the event, telling readers that they could order their kits by calling the museum office and to schedule an appointment to come to the event in order to learn how to use the kit.*

*Mark was so excited! The board meeting was next Tuesday and he couldn't wait to tell the others what he had accomplished!*

## What Could Have Been Done?

It's possible that Mark was not ready for board service. The fact that he felt empowered to move forward with a brand-new program just because he had joined the board indicates that he either had no previous board experience (and therefore did not understand that what he was doing was not the work of the board) or he may have previously served on a board of an organization in a much earlier cycle of organizational development (one where the board members did more hands-on work due to a lack of staff). The difference between Mark's role as a board member and his previous role as a volunteer should have been clarified for him.

## Solution Strategy: Now What?

The board chair needs to find a way to immediately undo what Mark has done in a manner that saves face for both the organization and for Mark. Perhaps the idea is a good one that could still be accomplished within the appropriate framework, but that needs to be a staff decision that meets the board's defined and agreed-upon organizational strategy and goals. It should also be made absolutely clear to Mark that the board is a governing board and that its job is to set the vision for the organization, and the paid staff members are responsible for suggesting and implementing the means in which the goals of the organization are achieved (mission fulfillment).

## After-the-Fact Conversation Starter

**Board chair:** *"Mark, your idea about doing a genealogy program is really wonderful, but we may not be able to do it. I feel bad telling you this after you have done so much research and work to set it up. You haven't been to enough meetings yet to understand that the work of our board may be different from what you might have assumed or experienced previously. We are not a hands-on board. We are fortunate to have a capable staff that is paid to do the jobs delegated to them. One of those specific jobs is developing programs within an approved annual operating budget. Our job as the board is to give the staff the big picture of what we hope will be achieved under our mission and then monitor their progress in developing the programs and necessary budgets to complete those programs, guarantee that their work is done legally, and ensure that our organization remains financially viable in the process. And we also help to friend-raise and fundraise.*

*"Do you have any questions about this? Would you be willing to work with me and the staff to figure out a way to postpone this program?"*

### BEHAVIOR: TELLS LIES

**Definition:** When a board member makes blatantly false statements or purposefully misleads other members of the board with the intent to deceive.

**Impact:** Dishonesty in any context causes lack of trust that is rarely possible to reverse. In the boardroom, lying will not only counteract seemingly good decisions and cause missed opportunities, but it could compromise the integrity of the organization.

**Case:** *When Melanie Mannan was being vetted for the board, the governance committee was extremely impressed with her background and experience. She had just moved to the area from Seattle where she had served on three major boards. One of them was the local Human Services board. While that organization didn't do exactly what our organization does, there were enough similarities to lead us to believe that Melanie would be a great fit.*

*Our development director, George, had researched the Gates Foundation and found that last year they had given a large grant to the Human Services organization in Seattle. We all thought that Melanie must be familiar with that. We were going to see Melanie the next day at the board meeting, but before that we asked George if he would call the Human Services organization and see if he could get some information about the program that the Gates Foundation had funded.*

*Well, you can imagine our surprise when George reported back that he inadvertently discovered that Melanie had never served on that board! They didn't even know who Melanie was! Then we did a little more checking and we found out that Melanie had not served on either of the other two boards she noted on her vita.*

### Solution Strategy: Now What?

The need for honesty should be common knowledge in any professional situation (or personal for that matter), especially when the success of an entire organization is at stake. Proper orientation could not have prevented this from happening — there is no ignorance or mistake to claim when being dishonest.

It is hard to conceive of any other outcome than removing individuals who are caught in a lie (or in this case, not accepting her onto the board in the first place). Each board should have a well-crafted clause in the bylaws that includes removal for dishonest behavior.

## INEFFICIENT BOARD DISCUSSIONS

The following behaviors divert the attention of the board's discussions during meetings and display an inability or unwillingness to take part in an informed debate. There is a continuum of board member contribution and when individual board members either overfunction or fail to contribute as expected, board meetings can feel like a waste of time, or at the very least won't accomplish what could be accomplished. Some or all of the following measures could be taken to prevent the behaviors from forming:

- All board members should have set term limits for their service (or at the very least, for the evaluation of service prior to renewal). If anything, this will mean there is an end date in site for difficult behavior.

- Governance committee members should be particularly aware during initial conversations with a prospective board member. If someone is not a good listener in an interview or informal introduction, chances are he or she won't be in the boardroom either.

Some of the behaviors below suggest more specific preemptive solutions and all will require additional action. Keep the suggestions on the previous page in mind as you read the specific cases and their solution strategies.

## BEHAVIOR: IS HIGH MAINTENANCE

**Definition:** When a board member expects constant and sometimes inappropriate attention, including unsuitable demand for staff support.

**Impact:** The high-maintenance board member can be simply a nuisance or a real hindrance. He or she can interrupt the focus of meetings, create an uneven team environment, be energy-draining for other board members and staff, and interrupt workflow and internal order.

**Case:** *Bonnie Bright was a great board member in so many ways. She was well respected and connected in the community. She was a great cheerleader, motivating others to support the cause. She followed through on assignments. She had the financial resources to make a difference and served as a role model for other board members and friends in the community in making financial contributions. But Bonnie took an enormous amount of time and attention. If she wasn't recognized at an event, she would stir things up until she was. If she didn't feel she was thanked enough, she would pout. If someone from the organization hadn't called her for a week or so, she would call to ask why. It seemed like the more attention she was given, the more attention she craved. The other board members and staff were becoming exhausted by the energy they had to expend to support this one person's ego.*

### Solution Strategy: Now What?

Because boards are made up of all kinds of people with many different characteristics and idiosyncrasies, sometimes this is the price one pays. Potential for this kind of behavior may not become apparent until it presents itself (in other words, it may be unavoidable). And, when the community is small, and there are only so many board candidates to pick from, it's almost impossible to find a board member without flaws. If Bonnie is the toast of the town, her service on the board may be critical to community acceptance of the organization. What are the other circumstances involved? Does Bonnie have a leadership position on the board?

After doing the Ben Franklin balance sheet — totaling up the pros and the cons of Bonnie's contributions to the board — the board chair and members of the governance committee should determine whether "living with it" is the best course of action. Is Bonnie's behavior actually preventing necessary work from being done? Or is it just time-consuming and irritating? If it is the latter, this may be a case of "do what it takes" until her term is up. The board is obviously benefiting from Bonnie's commitment, enthusiasm, thorough work, and connection with the community. But even "doing what it takes" could involve a fellow board member's well-intentioned attempt to talk to Bonnie about her behavior, rather than the group just accepting the troublesome situation. If it is the former, a serious intervention needs to take place.

### After-the-Fact Conversation Starter

One strategy would be to ask for cooperation indirectly:

**Board chair:** *"Bonnie, I need your help. Our meetings have become somewhat unfocused and seem to go on and on. People are so stretched for time yet we seem to spend a lot of energy and attention on the niceties rather than substance and forward direction. Our board members walk out of meetings wondering if they've just wasted their time rather than feeling pumped up about our work. Also, we seem to request a lot of attention and support from the staff that might be better spent on raising money for the organization or improving our programs."*

**Bonnie:** *"I'm not sure I see what you mean."*

**Board chair:** *"Well, for example, at the last meeting, we took almost an hour to acknowledge the accomplishments surrounding our last benefit. I do agree that celebrating successes and thanking people are very important, but I'm wondering if we might be able to do this in a more productive and time-efficient way so that we can use our board meetings to focus on planning.*

*"It occurs to me that if you and I model the right behaviors we might head off some problems at the pass. You are such a strong role model for the rest of the board. Would you be comfortable speaking up and, with me, steering the agenda this way?"*

Another strategy would be to confront the behavior head on:

**Board chair:** *"Bonnie, we have a problem. May I be frank with you?"*

**Bonnie:** *"Of course. What's up?"*

**Board chair:** *"I know you are greatly valued on the board and everyone actively acknowledges how much you contribute to the work we do. But, looking back over the course of the past year, I feel that we haven't been able to focus on accomplishing ongoing work because the board and staff dedicate a lot of time and attention to your phone calls or visits to the office. It occurs to me that maybe you think you need to do more than you should…"*

With sincerity and empathy, and *without* investing ego on the part of the initiator, the impact of Bonnie's neediness on the board and staff should be brought to her attention. This direct conversation between Bonnie and the board chair could be successful in two ways: It could give Bonnie a little of the one-on-one attention she is looking for and serve as an opportunity to stroke her ego, acknowledging her valuable work and support; and at the same time, providing a graceful and subtle "warning" may help Bonnie realize that her behavior is only harming her favor among other board and staff members.

### BEHAVIOR: MONOPOLIZES CONVERSATIONS

**Definition:** When someone feels compelled to offer his or her opinions on every subject, leaving no room for others to speak; and/or, when the individual feels it necessary to recap every discussion.

**Impact:** The board member who monopolizes conversations is more than just irritating to the rest of the group. As seen in other behaviors, these actions prevent others from contributing to brainstorming, strategic discussions, or intense deliberations, which leads to weakened decision making and diminishes the value of the rest of the board's insight and expertise. This troublesome board member's voice also becomes compromised in the end: Even when he or she has something good to offer, it gets tuned out by the rest of the group who is tired of dealing with someone who thinks his or her opinion is more valuable.

**Case:** *Monte Morris was not looking forward to going to today's board meeting. As board chair, he had been approached separately by several board members over the past few months and each had expressed concerns about Stan's interpersonal skills. Since coming on the board last year, Stan had not been the best "team member." It was clear that Stan somehow felt the need to offer his thoughts and suggestions on each and every issue that came up to the board. Even when points had already been clearly stated, Stan felt he needed to restate those points in his own words. One board member told Monte, "It's almost like Stan has this psychological need to hear himself talk!"*

### Solution Strategy: Now What?

It is the board chair's role to control this kind of behavior. In dealing with one board member who uses up all of the "talking time," the board chair needs to start out by having a one-on-one conversation with the person. He or she may not realize that this behavior has become troublesome to the rest of the board. More than anything, the board member may think he or she is being helpful by restating others' thoughts in clearer language or by contributing what he or she believes to be great insight from relevant experience. If the board chair approaches the issue delicately, and brings specific examples to the conversation in order to clearly illustrate the behavior and its effects, the board member may be open to suggestions for change and, at worst, be a little bit embarrassed.

If the board member has trouble grasping the problem, the board chair may need to run meetings a little differently and force the entire group to follow stricter procedures during meeting time. Each person may be required to "pass the torch" after a specific amount of time, and the next person may only speak once the torch is in his or her hand. The board chair may need to take responsibility for moderating each turn if the torch ends up back in the same hand over and over again.

In an effort to remind the group of the importance of "hearing" what others have to say and making room for equal contribution, the board chair could also facilitate board development sessions on the subject of active listening. Active listening is listening in a reflective way, which indicates an attempt to understand what another person is saying. It uses the process of paraphrasing back to clarify what someone has said or to assist someone else in understanding the correct message, context, and intent.

### BEHAVIOR: SITS SILENTLY

**Definition:** When a member of the board fails to voice his or her opinions or contribute to group discussions in any way.

**Impact:** This person was obviously brought on the board for a good reason. When the board member does not participate, the rest of the board misses out on his or her potentially valuable knowledge and insight. In the rare occasion that this board member does speak up, his or her voice may be too quickly overlooked or dismissed. Ultimately, a silent board member is taking the place of someone else who could be more active on the board.

**Case:** *Elaine Eby had served on the board with Jeff Jefferson for almost three years. Elaine had such admiration and respect for Jeff. Whenever he offered his input in a discussion at a meeting, it was always very clear and well thought out. Usually, whatever he had to say was one of the most valuable pieces of information the group would get about any given topic. However, Elaine was deeply concerned that Jeff didn't speak up more. Often there were two or three meetings in a row where Jeff never said a word!*

**Solution Strategy: Now What?**

There are many possible reasons for a board member's hesitation to speak out during board meetings. This person may feel any of the following:

- insecurity or discomfort when speaking in public

- the contributions of others are more worthwhile than his or her own

- everything that should be said has been said already

- others are dominating the discussion to such an extent that the person doesn't want to compete

It may be beneficial for the board chair to have an informal, one-on-one conversation with the quiet board member — just to be sure there aren't any deeper problems or concerns. If this person is holding back due to dominating board members in the room or a big-picture concern regarding the board or organization as a whole, it's necessary for the board chair to know what the issues are and do something about them. If, however, it is a matter of shyness or passivity, the board chair should reassure the board member that his or her contribution is absolutely necessary, wanted, and valued, and then find ways to draw participation out of each and every board member. Simple presence is not enough in the boardroom.

The board chair could and should make it a point to require group discussion at each meeting, literally going around the room and asking each person to share thoughts, concerns, or suggestions:

**Board chair:** (in next board meeting) *"The next topic on our agenda is whether or not we should think about changing our location in order to reach and serve more clients. I'm going to ask each of us to share in just a few words how he or she feels about this. For now, we won't react to each other's thoughts just yet; we'll just make our individual comments and record them. Then, we'll open it up for discussion and see where we have consensus and where we have disagreement. Let's start with Sharon and go right around the table."*

Additionally, providing board members with the tools to make personal insights, such as the Meyers-Briggs Type Indicator, would also help. This and other tools are helpful for each board member individually and for the team as a whole, so that board members get to know one another on a more personal level and gain a better understanding of how each person works best in a group atmosphere. Sometimes the necessary give and take in the boardroom is something that requires careful observation, personal understanding, and finesse.

# Chapter 4: Misfits and Delicate (but Troublesome) Circumstances

Rather than addressing specific behaviors, as in Chapters 2 and 3, this chapter covers challenges tied to specific positions, producing unacceptable *actions* that may lead to chronically troublesome behaviors. These scenarios are considered "special cases," both because they do not fall neatly into the other categories, and more so because the reactions to each require exceptional understanding and greater management. The unique troubles covered below include illegal activity, personal challenges, and founder's syndrome, as well as what to do when the troublesome board member is the board chair or the chief executive.

## ILLEGAL ACTIVITY

The illegal activity of a board member in fulfilling his or her responsibilities is rare; but, when it does occur, it will have more damaging effects on the organization than any other troublesome behavior.

Illegal activities can happen for a variety of reasons in many different contexts or settings. Some examples are as follows: when there is no paid staff and a board member handles the finances of the organization, and is misappropriating funds; a board member uses organizational funds in some way for personal benefit; a board member is charged with sexual harassment; or a board member participates in a campaign for a political candidate as a representative of the organization. Also rare, but more prevalent than board member illegal activity, is chief executive or staff illegal activity.

Regardless of the offender, the board, as the keeper of the public trust, is still liable for the entire organization and must take action to correct illegal behavior. These illegal acts can be nothing less than devastating to nonprofits, especially since they tarnish the organization's all-important reputation. In addition to having clear policies and safeguards, a prudent board should always be forthcoming with legal information. Fighting criminal activity is bad enough. Battling charges of a board cover-up can be disastrous.

### FRAUDULENT BEHAVIOR

The term fraud itself describes an act that is contrary to law. The act of fraud involves intentional deception resulting in harm to an organization, and usually also resulting in inappropriate or illegal gain to someone connected with the organization. Fraud can be committed by employees, board members, volunteers, members, clients, vendors, or anyone else connected to the nonprofit. Fraudulent situations can come in various forms, from the omission of assets on a balance sheet to an act of theft by an employee. Different kinds of fraud vary considerably in level of severity and illegality.

Most fraudulent individuals become more comfortable as they commit more illegal acts (thinking they will never be caught). As time goes by, the frequency and magnitude of the fraud usually increases until the person is caught or leaves the organization. This activity can cause financial loss, bad reputation, damaged relationships, negative publicity, loss of employees, loss of donors, litigation, difficulty in maintaining board members, and permanently damaged morale.

In general, fraud isn't always easy to spot. A watchful chief executive or senior staff can head off legal troubles tied to fraud by being aware of the warning signs, such as a disgruntled employee living above his or her means; an employee who never takes a vacation (possibly out of fear that he or she will be discovered while out of the office); and unusual variances on monthly financial statements. Boards must remember not to assume: "We'll catch it if something falls through the cracks." "Our auditors will find it." "Our internal controls will prevent it." And most of all, "Our employees won't steal." Unfortunately, these things happen (or fail to happen) more often than one may think, and the first step in solving the situation is by not getting caught up in an overly optimistic attitude.

Board members must take firm action to see that appropriate controls are in place, insisting on specific written policies and procedures. The board is responsible for making sure that the organization has a code of conduct for all employees and a clear conflict-of-interest policy and code of ethics for itself. It should see to it that there is only one style of financial statements used for budgeting, financial reporting, and external audit reports, allowing board members to better understand financial activity. The treasurer and finance committee should review the interim financial statements monthly.

Even after an act of fraud is discovered, some nonprofits fail to go public with the information for fear that negative publicity could ruin the organization. This response may actually encourage fraud: Other individuals might believe they have a free hand to take liberties. And, there is no guarantee that a leak to the public won't occur and the organization will be caught in a cover-up, causing an even greater upheaval in the community. Any criminal act must be reported.

After a fraudulent activity has occurred, the appropriate action will depend on the nature of the activity, the related laws, and the person's employment agreement (or relationship) with the organization. The board must consult with legal counsel to discuss the next steps and the extent of the fraud must be identified with a thorough investigation. In most cases, the police should be notified. Law enforcement will not only protect the organization presently, but will place the individual on record, preventing another organization in another state from suffering in the same way because of the same person.

It is very rare that an organization will choose *not* to terminate the staff or board member who acted illegally. With a sudden staff change and inevitable buzz surrounding the troublesome situation, it is important for the chief executive to communicate with the rest of the staff. He or she must be careful not to share too many details regarding the activity, but address the issue enough to squash inaccurate rumors, answer questions, and acknowledge concerns.

Finally, it is essential for the board to take care *not* to overreact. While it is the board's responsibility to do everything possible to address the situation and ensure sound internal controls in the future, the tendency is to clamp down into micromanagement and ultimately diminish the organization's ability to operate efficiently.

## SEXUAL HARASSMENT

Sexual harassment can be unwelcome sexual advances, requests for sexual favors, and other verbal or physical conduct of a sexual nature that disturbs the working environment. Often the perceptions of sexual harassment can be as offensive as the actual behavior.

Sexual harassment detrimentally affects the working environment. It creates fear, discomfort, and resentment among board members or staff, and may cause turnover. A charge of sexual harassment may put an organization at serious liability risk, compromise employee morale, and affect organizational reputation and good will.

Explicit steps must be taken when investigating any charge of sexual harassment. The specific ramifications of dealing with a sexual harassment incident that may involve an unpaid, volunteer board member and the subsequent handling of such a situation is best left to professionals. A human resources professional specializing in this area, as well as legal counsel, should be immediately consulted.

## POLITICAL POSITIONS THAT CREATE PROBLEMS FOR THE ORGANIZATION

Using one's position as a board member while campaigning for a political candidate or engaging in unapproved lobbying in the name of the organization can certainly be troublesome. A violation of the IRS regulations may result in the nonprofit losing its tax-exempt status and/or an obligation to pay excise taxes on the money improperly spent. Because there may be complicated subtleties depending on the particular situation and varying regulations of the IRS with regard to the legal status of nonprofits, dealing with this specific behavior cannot be adequately discussed within the covers of this book. If this is an area of concern with one of your board members, legal counsel should be sought.

# PERSONAL CHALLENGES

## EMOTIONAL ISSUES AND DEPENDENCY

When a board member suffers from a deeply personal issue — whether it be substance abuse, depression, anxiety, the loss of a loved one, or something else — it can deeply affect the boardroom, harming his or her ability to be of service or reflecting poorly on the organization's image.

Many times, this behavior manifests itself in subtle ways, such as extreme sensitivity to certain issues discussed or a lack of focus. Other times, it could cause disruptions or resentment if emotions get in the way of decision making or basic politeness during meetings. The behavior can build a barrier between the board member and the rest of the board due to both a hesitation on the board member's part in making social connections and an uncertainty in board members of how the troubled individual should be treated.

Behavior tied to these personal issues can cause a string of disappointments, most likely turning into other troublesome behaviors, some of which have been discussed in previous chapters: lateness, absence, lack of preparedness, lack of focus or ability to concentrate in meetings, mood swings, possible unethical or illegal behavior to support a dependency, or violence. Many times work performance is impaired and other board members must cover for the troubled individual, working harder because of his or her failures.

Due to all of the above, serious intervention is usually needed. A human resources professional should be confidentially consulted to determine the best course of action.

### UNIQUE ATTRIBUTES

In a less serious but perhaps broader category, there is a wide variety of personal attributes that an individual may not even be aware of. Some examples include bad breath, offensive body odor, habitual noises or ticks, inappropriate mannerisms, and even untraditional styles of interaction related to cultural, ethnic, or religious practices.

Individuals rarely see themselves as others see them; therefore, interactions affected by these personal attributes can be distracting and even unpleasant for the other board members. The end result may be disinterest in what the individual has to say, attempts to stifle the person's participation, or even the absence of fellow board members in order to avoid witnessing the troublesome characteristics.

In most cases, people sincerely want to know if they have an attribute that makes others uncomfortable or distracts the group. It may ease the news if a close friend discusses the issue with the board member. If this is not possible, the board chair will have to be the one. These conversations are best done in private and should be sensitive to the fact that this person might feel embarrassed by the confrontation and may not know how to respond.

This may also be the kind of behavior that results in the "just live with it" attitude. Some people have personal preferences or uncontrollable flaws regarding hygiene and other attributes; if others can find a way to see past the issue, the board will benefit just as much from the knowledge, experience, and commitment of the board member.

## FOUNDER'S SYNDROME

Founder's Syndrome can stem from the actual founder, from a dominant personality serving in a leadership role that has taken an organization through a significant period, or even from others regarding an individual who served as a leader in the past and who had an enormous influence on an organization. It can cause troublesome behavior in three areas: a controlling chief executive; a deferential board; and, if the founder becomes or remains a member of the board, a troublesome board member who threatens the board's relationship with the new executive and weakens the board as a decision-making body.

Founders are usually the first chief executives of an organization or the first chair of the board. In all cases, there is a natural feeling of ownership on the part of any founder, being the person or one of the few persons who realized a vision, found others to support and join it, and built a nonprofit organization from the ground up. Unfortunately, in response to this projected sense of ownership there is also resistance to change. The term "rubber-stamping" is often used in the same breath as founder's syndrome, meaning that the rest of the group automatically approves whatever the founder says or wants because of his or her passion and vision, and because sometimes it's just easier. This could cause individual troublesome board member behavior regarding the expectations of the founder, as well as a troublesome *board* that is unable and/or afraid to think independently in making appropriate decisions.

Rarely is it a good idea for the founder to step down from the chief executive position and move to the board. Organizational viability is threatened if the founder officially "leaves" a staff role but remains too involved; the reality is, the founder will not be there forever. Eventually the organization grows up and "goes away to college" — forming a new structure and moving forward from its original existence. With an unhealthy reliance on a founder, new leadership development is prevented, the advantages to a group or team process are lost, and the organization is locked in a certain phase of its lifecycle with no forward movement or growth.

In the same way, this transition to the board threatens the board's loyalty to the new chief executive who deserves a strong partnership with that board, and it may inadvertently invite the founder to supervise the organization's new manager. If the temptation to have an executive transition to the board does arise, it may cause the current board members to condone his or her behavior in the future because they are afraid to "be" something that doesn't involve him or her.

Or, conversely, once the founder leaves altogether, the board may swing too far into management to compensate for a perceived void. Finding the right balance following the transition of a founder is a real challenge for many organizations and their boards. Time, thought, strategy, and making the best use of the right people are all necessary when adjusting to new staff leadership. The board must be conscious of a daunting first step — taking a fresh look at the current needs of the organization and figuring out how to fill them.

## The Abilene Paradox

Founder's Syndrome brings up the perfect opportunity to reflect on the Abilene Paradox. The Abilene Paradox is when the limits of a particular situation force a group of people to act in a way that is directly the opposite of their actual preferences. It is a phenomenon that occurs when groups continue with misguided activities that no group member desires because no member is willing to raise objections. It was observed by management expert Jerry B. Harvey in his 1988 book, *The Abilene Paradox and Other Meditations on Management*. The name of the phenomenon comes from an anecdote in the book that Harvey uses to elucidate the paradox:

*On a hot afternoon visiting in Coleman, Texas, the family is comfortably playing dominoes on a porch, until the father-in-law suggests that they take a trip to Abilene (53 miles away) for dinner. The wife says, "Sounds like a great idea." The husband, despite having reservations because the drive is long and hot, thinks that his preferences must be out-of-step with the group and says, "Sounds good to me. I just hope your mother wants to go." The mother-in-law then says, "Of course I want to go. I haven't been to Abilene in a long time." The drive is hot, dusty, and long. When they arrive at the cafeteria, the food is as bad. They arrive back home four hours later, exhausted. One of them dishonestly says, "It was a great trip, wasn't it." The mother-in-law says that, actually, she would rather have stayed home, but went along since the other three were so enthusiastic. The husband says, "I wasn't delighted to be doing what we were doing. I only went to satisfy the rest of you." The wife says, "I just went along to keep you happy. I would have had to be crazy to want to go out in the heat like that." The father-in-law then says that he only suggested it because he thought the others might be bored.*

The group sits back, perplexed that they together decided to take a trip that none of them wanted. They each would have preferred to sit comfortably, but did not admit to it when they still had time to enjoy the afternoon.

The phenomenon may be a form of groupthink. It is easily explained by social psychology theories of social conformity and social cognition, which suggest that human beings often feel great disincentives to acting in a manner contrary to the trend of the group. Likewise, it can be observed in psychology that indirect cues and hidden motives often lie behind peoples' statements and acts, frequently because social disincentives may exist that preclude individuals from openly voicing their feelings or pursuing their desires.

The theory is often used to help explain extremely poor business decisions, especially notions of the superiority of "rule by committee." A technique mentioned in the study and/or training of management, as well as practical guidance by consultants, is the following: When the time comes for group members to make decisions, they should ask each other, "Are we going to Abilene?" to determine whether their decision is legitimately desired by the group's members or merely a result of this kind of groupthink.[9]

9. Wikipedia: http://en.wikipedia.org/wiki/abiline_paradox.

If the current founder does step down from the executive position and separate himself or herself appropriately from the organization, a consultant/facilitator can provide incredible value to the board with guidance and fresh perspective through a significant organizational transition. For example, frank discussions about the chief executive's current and future value to the organization, such as passion for the mission, institutional memory, fundraising ability, and the way his or her historic public persona is tied with the organization would be fruitful. These acknowledgments could be combined with open discussions about the new opportunities and possibilities without the executive at the helm. What activities could he or she stay involved in to capitalize on his or her valuable connection to the organization, while also allowing it to move on to the next step? Where does the organization want to go in this next stage of development and what kind of leadership is needed for that to happen? Is there a chance that the original mission or vision of the organization needs to change in order to adapt to the community's needs?

The executive may also benefit from transition coaching. Facing loss of control over a personal vision will generate a swarm of feelings, both about his or her determined new role and the need to accept the organization's necessary growth and change.

Having a leadership succession plan and process in place prior to the actual transition can contribute to a healthy future. In most cases, the board most likely has some advance notice that the time is coming for a leadership transition. Setting up a special task force to look at the specific issues involved is a necessary consideration.

Additionally, performance evaluations should be conducted on an annual basis. With a consistent and formal evaluation process, the board has a chance to take control over ensuring that the right chief executive is in place. And, it provides the board with an opportunity to give both positive and negative feedback to the chief executive, often asking for improvements or change in particular areas of performance.

## THE TROUBLESOME BOARD *CHAIR*

What happens if the troublesome behavior is coming from the board chair? First, it may be more difficult to recognize the behavior since the board chair is facilitating the group process. Board chair problems come in two varieties: 1) the board chair cannot run meetings effectively or interact with people appropriately (but somehow got voted into the position); and/or 2) the chair displays any of the previously discussed board member behaviors, which makes it extremely challenging since no one is in an obvious position to confront him or her.

---

### FOOD FOR THOUGHT

*"There is no one right style of leadership. At the end of the day, the winning chair is the one who ensures board integrity and maintains focus on achieving the mission of the organization."*

Ane Powers, Founder and Managing Partner, The White Hawk Group, Washington, DC

Overall, a troublesome board chair usually lacks leadership and fails to properly manage the board process. Over and over again throughout this book, it is crystal clear that the troublesome behaviors of a board member must be dealt with by the board chair. When the board chair fails to provide this necessary leadership and active management, troublesome behaviors are bound to develop in others as well.

Often, the individuals who assume the board chair position as leader of leaders may not have the experience to actually lead a group/team process. Does the board have a standard practice when grooming board members for leadership or vetting external candidates for officer positions? As part of the necessary succession planning and board development activities, a new board chair will be better prepared if provided with written resources in advance of the time he or she assumes the role. In addition, he or she may seek out learning or other professional development activities and ask the outgoing or immediate past chair to provide mentoring for a specific period of time.

Depending upon the nature of the troublesome behavior and whether there is a consistent pattern, it will be up to the executive committee or the governance committee to lead the intervention. Putting the chief executive in the uncomfortable position of dealing with a board chair's behavior is inappropriate and inadvisable, and simply is not his or her role to do so. If the governance committee has been tasked (as it should be) to lead board assessment — of individuals and the group — it will make the most sense for recommendations regarding a troublesome board chair to come from that committee.

One thing is for sure: These difficult conversations should not be one-on-one. A receiver attaches greater credibility to a small group of interveners than a single person. If the intervention is made by one intervener, it can be easily rationalized away by the receiver. And, if there is an unpleasant exchange or threatening behavior, there are no other witnesses present.

Sometimes, the board chair may take his or her position as leader *too* far, abusing the power of authority over the rest of the board and/or confusing his or her role with that of the chief executive. Situations like this may necessitate additional intervention by an external consultant to attempt to mediate an understanding and coach the board chair in his or her role as board *leader*, not board "boss" or staff manager. This is an expense the organization may not be willing to take (and, as some may think, should not have to) but if a domineering board chair is in the beginning of his or her term, the only choices would be to terminate the chair or live with it. Living with it for an extended period of time may do the entire organization a great deal of permanent harm. Termination would mean either asking the board chair to resign or potentially facing an ugly battle for which the basis of termination may be called into legal question. When this is the case, keeping documentation when issues arise and having appropriate language in the bylaws for the removal of a board member become absolutely critical.

While the definitions of leadership are endless, in Robert H. Rosen and Paul B. Brown's book, *Leading People*, they identified eight principles of successful leaders. A board chair should help to inspire the board team to develop **vision**. He or she should lead by example by having and earning **trust**. The board chair actively ensures **participation** by all through proper facilitation of meetings and other board processes. By helping to create a **learning** culture, the board chair will ensure that a governance committee exists and that its work will embrace continuing education, including board knowledge enhancement and skill development. The board chair will work hard to ensure that the board values and embraces the appropriate and needed **diversity** for mission fulfillment. He or she will challenge the board and staff as a whole to be **creative** in problem solving. Leading by example, the board chair will embody **integrity** and demand it of others. And, above all, by acknowledging that he or she is not only leading but also an active part of a team in serving a constituency, the board chair will take a stand in building **community**.

In the recruitment process or leadership succession planning phase, the governance committee needs to be mindful of specific objectives when considering a new chair of the board. Board chairs are most effective when they have the ability to

- Get along with and motivate a wide variety of people.

- Command respect from the rest of the team.

- Be confident in addressing troublesome behaviors.

- Facilitate the team process and lead it to group decision making.

- Listen.

All board members should be aware of the leadership and management qualities necessary for an effective board chair. When one or more of these qualities is compromised (or missing altogether) and result in troublesome behavior, other members of the board must have the courage to take necessary action. It is important to remember that leadership is a vested process. No one can be a leader unless it is with the consent of the group he or she is leading.

# Dealing with a Troublesome Chief Executive

Theoretically, the board has done due diligence in recruiting, interviewing, and onboarding the right candidate to serve as the chief executive. There are many factors to take into consideration and excellent resources to assist a board with this important task.

As with the troublesome board chair, the real trouble arises when the chief executive displays the behaviors discussed earlier in this chapter and in Chapters 2 and 3, or misunderstands his or her role of power. Other signs of a troublesome chief executive might include

- subordination

- lack of appreciation or use of board support

- poor working relationship with the board chair

- unresponsiveness

- withholding information

- excessive staff turnover

- dwindling contributions or earned income

- ineffective public relations

In many cases, the chief executive is running the board process instead of the board running the board process. The board chair and the chairs of each committee should run their respective meetings. The chief executive and other appropriate staff actively contribute to the development of board meeting agendas and provide support for the process, but board meetings are not the responsibility of the staff. The number one sign of a major problem is if the board chair and the chief executive are not working together, not even on the meeting agendas.

Decisions made by the board should be decisions of the entire group. The chief executive may prepare the information for consideration and will often be a part of the decision-making process or the discussions leading up to the decision, but ultimately it requires the consensus of the board.

However, given all of the above, boards cannot have performance, behavioral, or goal-oriented expectations of the chief executive unless those expectations have been communicated. The ongoing measurement of these expectations and prevention or discovery of troublesome behaviors is done through a formal, annual chief executive assessment process. If a chief executive is troublesome, the board has failed to fulfill one of its most important governance responsibilities.

Conducted properly, an assessment will indicate if there are behavioral issues that need to be addressed. If this is the case, the board may ask the chief executive to work with a development coach consultant (at the organization's expense upon the board's choosing of a coach). The coach will gather information regarding the chief executive's behaviors and performance — often through a 360 analysis, direct report input, peer input, or other self-awareness tools. The chief executive and the coach should clarify together the behaviors and issues to be discussed and improved, creating a set of deliverables. The coach's role is to help the chief executive understand that this is a "reality check," asking for answers to the following questions: Do you hear what others are saying? Can you make the needed changes? If so, how are you going to make these changes? If others do not see improvement during the coaching period, the troublesome behaviors or flawed performance simply may not be coachable.

Additionally, having a set time for closed executive session at every board meeting is extremely valuable. If it is done regularly, without the chief executive, then it provides a natural and nonthreatening forum for introducing sensitive subjects. Board members have an opportunity not only to informally discuss the chief executive if needed, but also to bring up peer-to-peer issues privately, apart from the staff. Unfortunately but realistically, this is also the time to remember and assert the fact that the board is the chief executive's boss. If board members are unhappy with performance and/or are not able to govern the organization because of a troublesome chief executive, it is up to them to make the necessary change and turn things around before troublesome becomes dangerous.

## FOOD FOR THOUGHT

Rachel Kraft, former development director at the Goodman Theatre in Chicago, and now executive director of the Lookingglass Theatre Company, offers a staff perspective about how boards govern. As far as she is concerned, even though the two theatres are dramatically different, she believes she has had the privilege of seeing two of the best in action.

She agrees that there are fundamental responsibilities of all nonprofit boards, but the boards of performing arts organizations are different — both from other boards, but also from each other. Performing arts, by their nature, are more experimental than the fine arts. Often, their boards attract members with a more entrepreneurial spirit. Still, within each performing arts organization there are going to be important distinctions. Comparing her previous theatre to her current theatre, she thinks that tailoring board process to the unique needs of the organization is critical.

*"The Goodman Theatre is a well-established leader on the Chicago cultural scene and certainly one kind of model for how multiple boards (governing, women's board) work together. Lookingglass, about to celebrate its 20th anniversary, is relatively younger. We have an artistic ensemble as stakeholders and while they aren't all actually on the governing board, their input and consensus is critical and the workings of the board reflect that exchange, especially with regards to strategic direction. Our board is just as involved but the systems are more fluid because of that additional element."*

To avoid troublesome behavior, Rachel believes that one of the most important aspects of a successful board/staff relationship is to keep the emphasis on building the relationship between the organization and the board member.

*"Hopefully my personal relationship with individual board members is good, but what it's really about is making sure that the staff is helping to facilitate the strongest relationship possible between the board member and the theatre to help us fulfill our mission. My threshold is high for all sorts of personalities when I know that the board member really believes in the organization and is giving it their all because of that. When you believe the motives are pure, the staff can channel all sorts of different energy for the good."*

Again, the most important job of the board is to ensure that the organization has strong and effective staff leadership. The hiring of the chief executive, his or her annual assessment, and effecting change when necessary must be embraced by the board. Ignoring this fundamental responsibility will put the organization in jeopardy.

# Chapter 5: We're Only Human

*If I could be you, if you could be me*
*For just one hour, if we could find a way*
*To get inside each other's mind*
*If you could see you through my eyes*
*Instead of your own ego I believe you'd be*
*I believe you'd be surprised to see*
*That you've been blind*
*Walk a mile in my shoes*
*Just walk a mile in my shoes*
*Before you abuse, criticize, and accuse*
*Then walk a mile in my shoes[10]*

## IN ANOTHER'S SHOES

A book like this would not be written unless with the following caveat: While we recognize that troublesome behaviors *do* exist and *will* interfere with the effective governance of a nonprofit board, the identification of the problem must be one with an end goal of seeking to *understand* that problem while offering possible solutions. The world would be better for all if everyone's work began with an attempt to build bridges instead of walls and an understanding that, on a fundamental level, we are all connected. It is important to look at this issue from a humanistic perspective. Behaviors are behaviors and people are people. Label the behavior, not the person.

The first step towards understanding and appropriately dealing with troublesome behaviors is to actively use the golden rule. It is best interpreted as saying: "Treat others only in ways that you're willing to be treated in the same exact situation." To apply the golden rule adequately, imagine yourself in the exact place of the other person on the receiving end of the action; consider what effect your words and actions have on the lives of others. With knowledge, imagination, and the golden rule, we can progress far in our moral thinking.

## WHO SAYS THERE IS A PROBLEM?

Board members are people too. Fear and denial are two of the most crippling feelings a person could have, regardless of the simplicity or severity of the situation. Many times, board members are too afraid to speak up and even acknowledge for the group that there is a troubling presence on the board. The thought, "I don't want to look like a troublemaker," could lead to the group's choice to ignore and work around an issue, a temptation discussed in previous chapters. But a board member has the right and the opportunity to articulate a sincere concern. In acknowledging or addressing a troublesome behavior, following appropriate channels and looking at the facts and

---

10. "Walk a Mile in My Shoes" © 1969 Sony/ATV Lowery Songs LLC. All rights administered by Sony/ATV Music Publishing, 8 Music Square West, Nashville, TN 37203. All rights reserved. Used by permission.

circumstances from all sides is essential. And, most of the time, the person will find that he or she is courageous in saying what everyone else is thinking.

Sometimes, however, there is a disagreement about the existence of a problem behavior. This is where denial usually fits in. The disagreement could be because someone simply does not want to believe there is a problem (even if it isn't he or she who is the cause) or because the person doesn't want to take responsibility for doing anything about it. In rare cases where someone might be trying to make a power grab, a different kind of denial may present itself. This could be because someone else has an ulterior motive that is served by the troublesome behavior; and therefore, he or she will not agree with the existence of such behavior.

The board chair and members of the governance committee should always be mindful of patterns. Removing anything personal, they may see if, over the course of several meetings, there is an emerging pattern showing that the group has not been able to work agreeably or efficiently. If the group process is constantly being compromised, then ask: Is there a consistent reason why? If that reason points to a pattern of behavior that points to an individual, then yes, there is a problem.

## HOLDING UP THE MIRROR

As shown with many of the solutions and conversation starters in previous chapters, most times all it takes is for the troublesome board member to be forced into realization. If an individual doesn't realize that he or she is offending or debilitating someone or something, it can't be corrected until he or she is made aware of the problem.

The initial strategy should always be to address directly, counsel, and coach for better behavior. Sometimes one finds that there is more to the behavior than someone just being difficult. It could be a board member in good conscience trying to bring up an elephant in the room. He or she could have a sincere concern about an organizational situation, condition, or consequence that may not be seen or dealt with by others. Or this person may be intentionally taking on the devil's advocate role, which can be a positive thing unless it is abused (intentionally or unintentionally) and expends too much time and energy by overchallenging the group consensus at every meeting. And again, it may just be that someone is just not aware that his or her behaviors are viewed as troublesome, especially when it is a pattern of behavior no one has ever addressed or because the individual has no other frame of reference.

Sometimes even after doing all of the preventative work and/or attempting the solutions that have been discussed, an individual just may not be able to effectively work as a team member or function in an appropriate manner as a board member. The kicker is: Personality and ego come into play in nonprofit board work in the same way they do in families, clubs, businesses, and other teams or group formations. If it isn't situational acting out, it could be a permanent character flaw.

# GOOD NIGHT AND GOOD LUCK

After all that's been said, it may just be that those who are not measuring up should simply be asked to step down. It is acceptable that individual board members who are up for term renewal would be assessed approximately six to nine months prior to nomination for a successive term. Some boards choose to have an *annual* assessment process and removal mechanism installed so that someone who isn't living up to expectations can be removed. If the conditions under which removal will be considered are spelled out and communicated in advance and then applied consistently, it becomes a reflective group process rather than a real or perceived personal indictment.

The governance committee is charged with assessment and recommendation regarding term renewal. These recommendations should be discussed with the board chair and with the individual board member in question. By the time it comes to the full board meeting, the final recommendation is known by all.

If there is a special situation in which a board member's behaviors are troublesome to the point of prompting review in between term renewals, the governance committee should convene in a timely manner to address the issue and make the recommendation for removal. This is necessary when the board member's behavior has been so egregious that keeping him or her on board would be against the organization's best interests and/or put the organization in financial or legal jeopardy; or, after a fair chance for change and understanding was given to the board member, but he or she didn't do anything to alter the behavior. Again, this determination should be made with deliberation and due process. An executive session could take place *without* the presence of the board member and then the full board must vote on the final decision for removal.

---

### FOOD FOR THOUGHT

*"The board shall have the authority to remove a board member who is found to be neglectful or unable to perform duties of a board member by the affirmative vote of two-thirds of the full board.*[11]*"*

---

Before taking the step to say goodbye, the proper mechanisms to do so must be in place. Actualization is contingent upon the pre-establishment of the written documentation and mechanisms established in the bylaws to do so. These policies for removal should have been read and understood by all board members upfront. Legal counsel should be consulted to ensure that the action of removal cannot be construed in anyway as libelous or slander.

Second, the governance committee needs to think through in advance how to "save face" for all involved in this uncomfortable situation — not only out of general

---

11. Carroll, John L. *Club Board Member's Guide: How To Become an Effective Member of Your Club Board.* Sarasota, FL: Pineapple Press, Inc., 2001. Page 184.

respect, but to save the organization from possible retaliation and to be successful in sending the departing board member off without resentment or a tarnished view of his or her experience on the board. Asking for a resignation and, if possible, finding another opportunity for the person to serve the mission (unless the problem is of an unethical or illegal nature) is the optimum way of saying goodbye.

As discussed previously, after removal, the board chair should initiate teamwork around the loss of a fellow board member. This process should not be overlooked in that it provides closure for the rest of the group, answers any unanswered questions or concerns, airs potential relief or pent-up feelings, and allows the board to start fresh when a new member joins the team.

---

**FOOD FOR THOUGHT**

*"Other board members were starting to be demoralized that this person was being carried. One other board member in particular (the board treasurer) really started having an issue with this person coming to the meetings, offering her opinions, but then not honoring her commitments. What's the most upsetting is how much energy it took. It took six months of energy that did nothing to move the organization forward. But now that it's resolved, I feel a renewal of energy and commitment to the organization."*

The person identified as Dan Devine (see page 36)

---

# Conclusion

The new discoveries (and resulting wonders) in quantum mechanics encourage each of us to think in terms of unfathomable possibilities. Many believe there is another major paradigm shift ahead for the human race. This shift will include a greater understanding and knowledge that we are all connected, that we are all one, and that life is eternal — an unprecedented melding of science and spirituality. That everything each of us thinks, does, or says, positive or negative, has an impact on the rest of us — a state of mutual coexistence for all time.

Could the historic role of philanthropy and serving on nonprofits be one of the stepping stones on the road to this paradigm shift? Do we (should we) give to live? Do the emotions of compassion and empathy exist so that we can eventually understand how truly connected we all are?

Working and living well requires meaning. There are few things as satisfying as using one's talents, skills, and experience to serve the public good. Yet, "…experience is necessary to add emotional belief to intellectual understanding."[12] It all comes down to human interaction and the building of relationships.

Wouldn't it be nice if someday, the need for formal philanthropy, the existence of nonprofit organizations, the giving of the haves to the have-nots, would not be necessary? Would not even be in the human frame of reference? That this could be

---

12. Brian L. Weiss, M.D.

so because our relationships with one another, stranger and friend, were strong, healthy, and compassionate?

Figuring out the cause of troublesome behavior in any context starts with compassion and understanding. Add some gentleness and kindness when addressing the conflicts and behaviors and we will all be closer to honoring the primary law of peaceful coexistence.

May it be so.

# Suggested Resources

## Organizational Web Sites

Association of Governing Boards of Universities and Colleges
www.agb.org

BoardSource
www.boardsource.org

The Center on Philanthropy at Indiana University
www.philanthropy.iupui.edu

Council on Foundations
www.cof.org

Donors Forum of Chicago
www.donorsforum.org

The Ethics Resource Center
www.ethics.org

Independent Sector
www.independentsector.org

National Council of Nonprofit Associations
www.ncna.org

The National Human Services Assembly
www.nassembly.org/nassembly

Society of Human Resources Management
www.shrm.org

Also see various individual state nonprofit associations.


## Publications

American Bar Association Coordinating Committee on Nonprofit Governance. *Guide to Nonprofit Corporate Governance in the Wake of Sarbanes-Oxley*. Chicago IL: American Bar Association, 2005.

Andringa, Robert C. and Ted W. Engstrom. *Nonprofit Board Answer Book*. Washington, DC: BoardSource, 2002.

Axelrod, Nancy R. *Chief Executive Succession Planning: The Board's Role in Securing Your Organization's Future*. Washington, DC: BoardSource, 2002.

Blanchard, Kenneth and Norman Vincent Peale. *The Power of Ethical Management*. New York: William Morrow and Company, 1988.

BoardSource. *Self-Assessment for Nonprofit Governing Boards*. Washington, DC: Board-Source, 1999.

BoardSource. *The Source: Twelve Principles of Governance That Power Exceptional Boards*. Washington, DC: BoardSource, 2005.

Carpenter, Brian L. "The Five Dysfunctions of Charter School Boards." National Charter Schools Institute. www.nationalcharterschools.org.

Carver, John. *Boards That Make a Difference: A New Design for Leadership in Nonprofit and Public Organizations*. Hoboken, NJ: John Wiley & Sons, 1997.

Chait, Richard P., William P. Ryan, and Barbara E. Taylor. *Governance as Leadership: Reframing the Work of Nonprofit Boards*. Co-published by John Wiley & Sons and BoardSource, 2005.

Connolly, Paul M. *Navigating the Organizational Lifecycle: A Capacity-Building Guide for Nonprofit Leaders*. Washington, DC: BoardSource, 2006.

Dietel, William M. and Linda R. Dietel. *The Board Chair Handbook*. Washington, DC: BoardSource, 2001.

Fisher, B. A. *Small Group Decision Making* (2nd ed.). New York: McGraw-Hill, 1980.

Flynn, Outi. *Meet Smarter: A Guide to Better Nonprofit Board Meetings*. Washington, DC: BoardSource, 2004.

Gladwell, Malcolm. *Blink: The Power of Thinking Without Thinking*. New York: Little, Brown and Company, 2005.

Hughes, Sandra R., Berit M. Lakey, and Marla J. Bobowick. *The Board Building Cycle: Nine Steps to Finding, Recruiting, and Engaging Nonprofit Board Members*. Washington, DC: BoardSource, 2000.

Ingram, Richard T. *Ten Basic Responsibilities of Nonprofit Boards*. Washington, DC: BoardSource, 2003.

Kurtz, Daniel L. and Sarah E. Paul. *Managing Conflicts of Interest: A Primer for Nonprofit Boards*. Washington, DC: BoardSource, 2006.

Lancaster, Lynne C. and David Stillman. *When Generations Collide: Who They Are. Why They Clash. How to Solve the Generational Puzzle at Work*. New York: HarperCollins Publishers, 2002.

Lawrence, Barbara and Outi Flynn. *The Nonprofit Policy Sampler, Second Edition*. Washington, DC: BoardSource, 2006.

Lieberman, David J. *How To Change Anybody*. New York: St. Martin's Press, 2005.

Mintz, Joshua and Jane Pierson. *Assessment of the Chief Executive: A Tool for Nonprofit Boards, Revised*. Washington, DC: BoardSource, 2005.

Moyers, Richard L. *The Nonprofit Chief Executive's Ten Basic Responsibilities*. Washington, DC: BoardSource, 2006.

Rosen, Robert H. and Paul B. Brown. *Leading People: The Eight Proven Principles for Success in Business*. New York: Penguin Books, 1996.

Seashore, Charles N., Edith Whitfield Seashore, and Gerald M. Weinberg. *What Did You Say? The Art of Giving and Receiving Feedback*. Columbia, MD: Bingham House Books, 1992.

Solomon, Muriel. *Working With Difficult People*. London, England: Prentice-Hall International (UK), 1990.

Tesdahl, D. Benson. *The Nonprofit Board's Guide to Bylaws: Creating a Framework for Effective Governance*. Washington, DC: BoardSource, 2003.

*The BoardSource Governance Series*. Washington, DC: BoardSource, 2003. Includes *Ten Basic Responsibilities of Nonprofit Boards, Financial Responsibilities of Nonprofit Boards, Structures and Practices of Nonprofit Boards, Fundraising Responsibilities of Nonprofit Boards, Legal Responsibilities of Nonprofit Boards, The Nonprofit Board's Role in Setting and Advancing the Mission, The Nonprofit Board's Role in Planning and Evaluation, How To Help Your Board Govern More and Manage Less*, and *Leadership Roles in Nonprofit Governance*. (Booklets also sold separately)

Weiss, Brian L. *Many Lives, Many Masters*. New York: Simon & Schuster, 1988.

Wheatley, Margaret J. *Leadership and the New Science: Learning About Organizations from an Orderly Universe*. San Francisco: Berrett-Koehler Publishers, 1992.

Zemke, Ron, Claire Raines, and Bob Filipczak. *Generations at Work: Managing the Clash of Veterans, Boomers, Xers, and Nexters in Your Workplace*. New York: American Management Association, 2000.

# About the Author

Katha Kissman is a senior governance associate consultant with BoardSource and provides interim leadership and organizational development consulting for a wide variety of organizations nationally and internationally.

Previously, Ms. Kissman served as Leadership America's executive director in 1996 and 1997, and then again as president and CEO in 2000 and 2001. She helped found the American University of Kuwait's Continuing Education Center in 2004 and the American University of Sharjah's Continuing Education Center in the United Arab Emirates in 1998 and 1999. Ms. Kissman also held previous leadership positions as the director of training and organizational development at the national headquarters of Volunteers of America, managing director of the Helen Hayes Award-winning Round House Theatre, and assistant managing director for Living Stage at Arena Stage.

Ms. Kissman currently serves or has served on the boards of the Office Depot Business Women's Council, IONA Senior Services, the African Continuum Theatre Company, the Trans-Arab Research Institute, the New Buffalo Railroad Museum, Leadership Montgomery, the Berrien County Economic Development Commission, the Harbor Country Chamber of Commerce, the Maryland State Arts Council, the Cultural Alliance of Greater Washington, Greentree Shelter for Women, NOW, and Hexagon.

For further information or to contact her, please visit her Web site at www.kathakissman.com.